Holidays
in the U.S.A.

An Interactive ESL Reader

Catherine Porter

Elizabeth Minicz

Carole Cross

ScottForesman

A Division of HarperCollins*Publishers*

We dedicate this book to our families—especially Paul, Wojciech, Eric, Christa, and Ian—for giving us a lifetime of holidays.

Photo Credits

Unless otherwise acknowledged, all photos are the property of Scott, Foresman. If more than one photo appears on a page, abbreviations are as follows: (t) top, (b) bottom.

p. 9, Elliott Erwitt/Magnum Photos; p. 11, AP/Wide World; p. 25 (t), Mount Vernon by William Russell Birch; p. 25 (b), New Salem Village; p. 28, Robert Llewellyn; p. 35, Brian Seed/TSWClick Chicago; p. 57, Dennis Kucharzak; p. 59, Photo Edit; p. 65, Jean-Claude LeJeune; p. 75, Brent Jones; p. 91, Library of Congress; p. 99, from engraving "Columbus Landing at Hispaniola" by Theodore DeBry; p. 107, Art Pahlke; p. 115, Don and Pat Valenti; p. 125, AP/ Wide World; p. 133, Gabe Palmer/The Stock Market; p. 135, The Bettmann Archive; p. 142, The Museum of the City of New York; p. 143, Gabe Palmer/The Stock Market; p. 152, Savage/The Stock Market.

Cover photos: (background) Chicago Photographic Company, (front) Bob Daemmrich, (back) Roy Morsch/The Stock Market.

ISBN 0-673-24979-4

1 2 3 4 5 6 - DBH - 96 95 94 93 92 91

Contents

About This Book

Holidays in the U.S.A. is part of a three-book series of high-interest, interactive readers for high-beginning adult or young adult students of English as a Second Language. The other two books in the series are *Places to Know in the U.S.A.*—in which students become familiar with places in the United States of historical, geographical, and cultural significance—and *Living in the U.S.A.*, in which students learn about unique features of everyday life in the United States.

In *Holidays in the U.S.A.*, students develop their reading, writing, listening, and speaking skills as they are introduced to the customs and backgrounds of U.S. holidays.

Solidly grounded in psycholinguistic reading theory, *Holidays in the U.S.A.* teaches students to interact with the printed word to "make meaning" of a text. Prereading and postreading activities develop students' prediction and confirmation skills and teach them to draw on *all* their knowledge (linguistic and contextual) when reading in a second language. Interaction and discussion activities provide an important bridge between silent reading and oral interaction in English. Writing activities and the singing of popular American songs further balance skill development.

Although the chapters are arranged chronologically according to the calendar year, they do not increase in difficulty and can therefore be used in any order. You will probably want to use the book for supplemental work whenever a holiday occurs.

How to Teach the Chapters

Each chapter has the following sections: Before You Read, the reading passage, Understanding New Words, Understanding What You Read, Before You Continue, Talk About It, and Write. Thirteen of the chapters also contain the section Let's Sing. The following instructions for using the components are suggestions only; adapt the activities as necessary to match your students' levels and needs.

Before You Read

Have your students open their books to the photograph or photographs beginning the chapter. Conduct a class discussion based on the picture and the questions below it. While you may choose to steer the discussion toward the holiday, accept all guesses as possible answers. Write the guesses on the board, if desired. Have students write their personal guesses on the lines.

The goal of the prereading discussion is threefold: (1) to engage students' background knowledge and focus students on the topic at hand, (2) to elicit/introduce relevant vocabulary, and (3) to instill in students curiosity and a desire to read. It is important that students do not turn the page and read ahead before the entire class has finished writing their guesses on the lines.

Reading Passage

Have the students read the passage silently a few times. Encourage them to underline unfamiliar vocabulary. If you have students with limited literacy skills, reading the story aloud to them after they have tried it on their own can aid comprehension.

Note, however, that having individual students take turns reading aloud is not a recommended procedure. Oral performance in front of the class does not develop reading skills for either the performer or the listeners. Oral performance of a reading passage is merely a test of pronunciation and decoding skills and has little to do with reading development. For these reasons, having students read aloud is strongly discouraged.

Understanding New Words

There is no need to preteach vocabulary since the vocabulary exercises following each reading passage are designed to develop the students' ability to guess the meanings of new words from context. Because good readers are good guessers, encourage students to do these exercises without consulting a dictionary. The format of the exercises (same/different, paraphrasing, multiple choice) varies according to the difficulty of the new words. The number of choices in the multiple-choice exercises is intentionally limited to help students gain confidence in guessing the meanings of new words.

The words from the passage highlighted in the vocabulary exercises are those likely to pose difficulty for high-beginning learners of English. Depending on your students' level, you may need to adapt the vocabulary practice. With some beginning groups, for example, you may find it necessary to include additional practice with other words from the reading passage. With intermediate-level groups, you may choose to introduce additional, more challenging vocabulary.

Understanding What You Read

A calendar activity checks comprehension of when the holiday is celebrated and fosters graphical literacy skill development. The calendar activity is followed by comprehension exercises that provide both literal and inferential comprehension checks. Although the first answer is always provided, it is important to go over the instructions with the class and discuss the example before having students complete an exercise.

Students are instructed to work with a partner to complete the comprehension activities. Pairing students provides an excellent opportunity for oral communication practice. To maximize use of English, pair students of different language backgrounds when possible.

In multilevel classes, it may be helpful to pair students of different ability levels when doing the comprehension exercises. To make the true/false exercises more challenging for students of higher ability, have students correct the false sentences.

Bringing in additional visual aids to help students understand American holiday customs is a good practice. Objects related to the holiday, personal photos, or pictures from newspapers and magazines can aid vocabulary development and comprehension. (You may choose to incorporate such realia into the prereading discussion— finding out what students know *first*—as well as into the postreading comprehension check.) For example, you can easily make a collage of old Christmas cards to illustrate relevant vocabulary and concepts. In addition, you can have students bring in holiday-related pictures from newspapers or magazines for further class discussion.

Before You Continue

Before moving on to the interaction and discussion activities, have students complete the two activities described in Before You Continue. Students confirm or revise their prereading predictions and then fill in the Holiday Chart in the back of the book. Filling in the chart can be a whole-class or individual activity and serves to summarize the key points of the reading passage. (The Holiday Expressions list on page 156 can assist students in filling out this chart.)

Talk About It

The pair and small-group activities in this section give students the opportunity to interact in English. The instructions are provided primarily for teacher reference; you will probably have to discuss or demonstrate each activity in some detail before having students work independently. It is also important to clarify and discuss any unfamiliar vocabulary before beginning an activity.

While the directions identify activities as pair or small group, many of the activities can be adapted to fit the needs of your class. Pair activities, for example, can be done in small groups, while small-group activities can be done in pairs. Adopt whatever activity type fits your class.

The interaction/discussion activities should always be followed by a whole-class discussion. The instructions usually tell students to share their answers and ideas with the class upon completion of an activity. It is best, however, to ask for volunteers. Because the content of a particular activity may be too personal for some groups of students, and because some students are very shy or reluctant to speak in front of the class, students should not be "forced" to share. Shyer students may be more inclined to participate if other students speak first.

Write

Because beginning students generally have limited control of vocabulary and syntax, the writing activities are quite structured. In some cases, these writing activities are personal, while in others, they provide additional vocabulary practice through brief cloze passages. As you are the best judge of your students' writing abilities, you may wish to adapt or extend the writing activities as necessary.

Let's Sing

Songs are a wonderful way to liven up the ESL classroom while developing language skills. Lyrics for songs are included for selected holidays. These songs were chosen because of their cultural significance and their easy-to-sing melodies. A cassette tape of the songs is available (see Cassette Tape on the next page).

Special Features of *Holidays in the U.S.A.*

Two items provide additional resources—the Answer Key, included in *Holidays in the U.S.A.*, and the Cassette Tape, available on order.

Answer Key

The Answer Key (see pages 157–166) provides answers for all the comprehension exercises. This is a helpful tool for teachers as well as for students using the book for self-study.

Cassette Tape

A cassette tape containing the 15 songs is available. The recordings have been selected for their clarity and appropriate pace for classroom use. A cassette insert provides the song lyrics and ideas for classroom presentation. The songs included are listed below.

Chapter 1	New Year's Eve and New Year's Day
	"Auld Lang Syne"
Chapter 2	Martin Luther King, Jr., Day
	"We Shall Overcome"
Chapter 3	Valentine's Day
	"Let Me Call You Sweetheart"
Chapter 5	St. Patrick's Day
	"Too-Ra-Loo-Ra-Loo-Ral"
Chapter 9	Memorial Day
	"When Johnny Comes Marching Home"
Chapter 10	Flag Day
	"You're a Grand Old Flag"
Chapter 11	Independence Day
	"The Star-Spangled Banner"
	"America the Beautiful"
Chapter 12	Labor Day
	"Sixteen Tons"

We wish to thank the following reviewers for sharing their expertise with us and for offering many helpful suggestions.

Sharron Bassano
Santa Cruz Adult School
Santa Cruz, California

Cheryl Kirchner
Milwaukee Area Technical College
Milwaukee, Wisconsin

Dr. Julia Spinthourakis
State of Florida
Department of Health and Rehabilitation Services
Tallahassee, Florida

We also wish to thank Carolyn Bohlman, for field-testing selected chapters; Dennis Terdy, for being a great boss and friend; Elaine Goldberg and Phil Herbst, for their eagle eyes and expert editing skills; and Roseanne Mendoza, for expecting us to give it our all!

BEFORE YOU READ

Talk about this photograph. Guess the answers to the questions
below. Write your guesses on the lines.

1. What are these people doing? _____

   _____

2. Why are some people wearing hats? _____

   _____

3. What time is it? _____

   _____

Now turn the
page and read.

New Year's Eve and New Year's Day

It is 11:59 P.M. on December 31. In just a minute, New Year's Day begins with a bang! Horns and noisemakers blow. People drink champagne. People kiss and hug each other. They say, "Happy New Year!" Everyone says good-bye to the old year and hello to the new one.

New Year's Eve is December 31. It is not a national holiday, so people often go to work on this day. But in the evening, many people go to parties. They stay up late and wait for the new year. They eat, drink, and dance. The people in the picture are at a New Year's Eve party. Some parties are at home. Other parties are at restaurants. In New York City, thousands of people wait outside in Times Square on New Year's Eve. They celebrate the new year with a lot of noise.

January 1 is New Year's Day. It is a national holiday, so most people don't have to go to work. Most people have a quiet day with family or friends. Some people have headaches because they drank too much alcohol the night before. Many Americans are concerned about drinking and driving. Drinking and driving is dangerous and illegal. On New Year's Eve, many cities have free buses and taxis so people don't have to drive.

Many Americans watch television on New Year's Day. In the morning, there are parades on TV. After the parades, there are college football games. One popular game is the Rose Bowl game in California. Millions of football fans watch this game.

On January 1, people think about the new year. Many people make resolutions. They decide to make changes in their lives. Some people promise to exercise more. Some decide to stop smoking. Others decide to lose weight. If people don't keep their New Year's resolutions, they can try again next year!

UNDERSTANDING NEW WORDS

Take turns reading these pairs of sentences with a partner. Is the meaning of the sentences the same or different? Decide with your partner. Circle SAME or DIFFERENT.

1. New Year's Day begins with a **bang.**

   New Year's Day begins with a lot of noise.

   (SAME)   DIFFERENT

2. Many Americans are **concerned** about drinking and driving.

   Many Americans are worried about drinking and driving.

   SAME   DIFFERENT

3. Drinking and driving is dangerous and **illegal.**

   Drinking and driving is dangerous, but it is not against the law.

   SAME   DIFFERENT

4. Millions of football **fans** watch the Rose Bowl game on New Year's Day.

   Many lovers of football watch the Rose Bowl game on New Year's Day.

   SAME   DIFFERENT

5. Many people make **resolutions** to exercise more in the new year.

   Many people promise to exercise more in the new year.

   SAME   DIFFERENT

UNDERSTANDING WHAT YOU READ

When Is the Holiday?

Fill in the year. Then write the dates for December and January. Circle New Year's Eve and New Year's Day.

December 19 _____

Sun.	Mon.	Tues.	Wed.	Thurs.	Fri.	Sat.

January 19 _____

Sun.	Mon.	Tues.	Wed.	Thurs.	Fri.	Sat.

New Year's Eve or New Year's Day?

Take turns reading these sentences with a partner. Is each sentence about New Year's Eve or New Year's Day? Decide with your partner. Put an X under NEW YEAR'S EVE or NEW YEAR'S DAY.

		NEW YEAR'S EVE	NEW YEAR'S DAY
1.	It is a quiet day.	_____	___X___
2.	It is a national holiday.	_____	_____
3.	People go to parties.	_____	_____
4.	There is a lot of noise.	_____	_____
5.	Many people watch football games on TV.	_____	_____
6.	People make New Year's resolutions.	_____	_____
7.	People stay up late.	_____	_____
8.	People drink champagne.	_____	_____

True or False?

Take turns reading these sentences with a partner. Is each sentence true or false? Decide with your partner. Put an X under TRUE or FALSE.

		TRUE	FALSE
1.	Many cities have free transportation on New Year's Eve.	X	
2.	Drinking on New Year's Eve is illegal.		
3.	On January 1, people think about the new year and make resolutions.		
4.	If people don't keep their New Year's resolutions, they go to jail.		
5.	New Year's Eve is noisier than New Year's Day.		

Understanding Sentences with Because

Take turns reading these sentences with a partner. Decide together how to finish each sentence. Cross out the letter of the answer. Then write the letter on the line.

1. People go to parties and stay up late on December 31 __c__

   a. because they want to make changes in their lives.

2. Most people don't go to work on January 1 _____

   b. because they don't want people to drink and drive.

3. Some people have headaches on New Year's Day_____

   ~~c.~~ because they are waiting for the new year.

4. Many cities have free buses and taxis on New Year's Eve _____

   d. because they drank too much alcohol the night before.

5. People make New Year's resolutions _____

   e. because it is a national holiday.

BEFORE YOU CONTINUE

- Look at your guesses on page 1. Were you right?
- Now fill in New Year's Eve and New Year's Day on the Holiday Chart on page 153.

TALK ABOUT IT

Talk to a partner about last year. Ask these questions and write your partner's answers on the lines. Then share the answers with the class.

Partner's Name: _____

1. Was last year good or bad for you? _____

2. What was one good thing about last year? _____

   _____

3. What was one bad thing about last year? _____

   _____

4. What is one thing you want to do in the new year? _____

   _____

WRITE

On New Year's Day, many Americans make resolutions for the new year. Read Pepe's New Year's resolutions.

1. I will stop smoking.

2. I will exercise three times a week.

3. I will lose 10 pounds this year.

Now write three things you want to do in the new year. Then share your resolutions with the class.

1. _____

2. _____

3. _____

LET'S SING

A poet from Scotland, Robert Burns, wrote this song about 200 years ago. Americans often sing this song at midnight on New Year's Eve.
Some of the words are difficult to understand because they are not English. They are Older Scottish. *Auld Lang Syne* means "old days gone by." People say good-bye to the old year when they sing this song.

Auld Lang Syne

Should old acquaintance be forgot
And never brought to mind?
Should old acquaintance be forgot
And days of Auld Lang Syne?

For Auld Lang Syne, my dear,
For Auld Lang Syne,
We'll take a cup of kindness yet,
For Auld Lang Syne.

For Auld Lang Syne, my dear,
For Auld Lang Syne,
We'll take a cup of kindness yet,
For Auld Lang Syne.

2

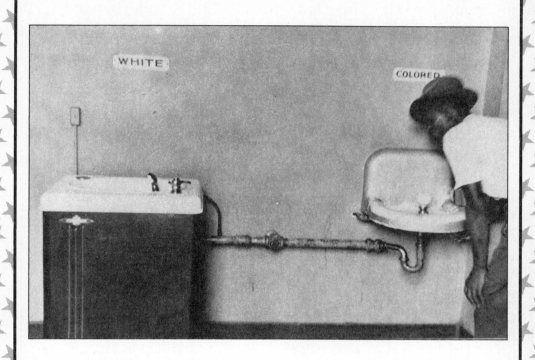

BEFORE YOU READ

Talk about this photograph. Guess the answers to the questions below. Write your guesses on the lines.

1. Who is this person? _____

   _____

2. What do the signs mean? _____

   _____

3. How does the person feel? _____

   _____

Now turn the page and read.

9

Martin Luther King, Jr., Day

The black man in the picture is drinking from a water fountain. It is 1955. There is a sign COLORED on the drinking fountain. For many years, black Americans did not have the same rights as white Americans. Drinking fountains and rest rooms had WHITE or COLORED signs. African Americans had to sit in the backs of buses. Many restaurants did not serve food to black people. In some places, black children and white children did not go to the same schools. Many African Americans could not vote. They had trouble getting good jobs.

A young black man from Georgia became angry. His name was Dr. Martin Luther King, Jr. He wanted equal rights for all Americans. He worked hard to make people's lives better. He led many peaceful demonstrations. One important demonstration was in 1963. Dr. King gave a speech in Washington, D.C., at the Lincoln Memorial. There were 250,000 people there. You can see Dr. King talking to the people in the picture on the next page. He told them,

> I have a dream . . . that one day little black boys and girls will join hands with little white boys and white girls and walk together as sisters and brothers.

One year later, in 1964, Dr. King received the Nobel Peace Prize. In 1968, a white man assassinated Dr. King. When Dr. King died, he was only 39 years old.

Dr. King's dream of peace and better lives for all Americans is alive today. In 1983, his birthday became a national holiday. On the third Monday in January, many Americans remember Martin Luther King, Jr. Students study about him. People listen to speeches and think about equal rights.

Life for African Americans is better today than it was in 1955. But there are still many problems. Dr. King's dream is still a dream.

Martin Luther King, Jr., speaks to marchers from the steps of the Lincoln Memorial, Washington, D. C.

UNDERSTANDING NEW WORDS

Take turns reading these pairs of sentences with a partner. Is the meaning of the sentences the same or different? Decide with your partner. Circle SAME or DIFFERENT.

1. There is a sign **COLORED** on the drinking fountain.

   Only black people can drink from this fountain.

   (SAME)   DIFFERENT

2. Martin Luther King, Jr., wanted **equal rights** for all Americans.

   Martin Luther King, Jr., wanted all Americans to have the same rights and freedoms.

   SAME   DIFFERENT

3. Martin Luther King, Jr., led many **peaceful demonstrations.**

   When Dr. King led demonstrations, many people died.

   SAME   DIFFERENT

4. In 1968, a white man **assassinated** Dr. King.

   In 1968, a white man killed Dr. King.

   SAME   DIFFERENT

UNDERSTANDING WHAT YOU READ

When Is the Holiday?

Fill in the year. Then write the dates for January. Circle Martin Luther King, Jr., Day.

January 19 ___

Sun.	Mon.	Tues.	Wed.	Thurs.	Fri.	Sat.

True or False?

Take turns reading these sentences with a partner. Is each sentence true or false? Decide with your partner. Put an X under TRUE or FALSE.

		TRUE	FALSE
1.	For many years, black Americans did not have the same rights as white Americans.	X	
2.	Whites had to sit in the backs of buses.		
3.	A young black woman from Georgia became angry.		

4.   Martin Luther King, Jr., worked   _____   _____
hard to make people's lives better.

5.   On the third Monday in January,   _____   _____
only African Americans remember
Dr. King.

6.   Life for African Americans was   _____   _____
better in 1955 than it is today.

7.   Dr. King's dreams of peace and   _____   _____
better lives for all Americans is not
alive.

8.   There are still many problems for   _____   _____
black Americans today.

BEFORE YOU CONTINUE

- Look at your guesses on page 9. Were you right?
- Now fill in Martin Luther King, Jr., Day on the Holiday Chart on page 153.

TALK ABOUT IT

When Americans are angry about laws, they do many things to protest. Martin Luther King, Jr., led peaceful demonstrations to change laws. Some people write letters and make telephone calls to government leaders. Some people march in demonstrations.

    Interview a partner about the issues below. How important is each issue? Circle 1, 2, or 3. Would you protest against the issue? Put an X under **Yes** or **No**.

Partner's Name: _____

				Would you protest?	
ISSUE	1 Very Important	2 Important	3 Not Important	Yes	No
nuclear weapons	1	2	3		
pollution	1	2	3		
high gasoline prices	1	2	3		
high taxes	1	2	3		
high medical costs	1	2	3		
expensive public transportation	1	2	3		
other:	1	2	3		

Which three issues are the most important to your partner? Share your partner's answers with the class.

1. _____

2. _____

3. _____

WRITE

Read the story and write in the missing words. Look at the words in the box below the story if you need help.

For many years, _____*black*_____ Americans did not have the
                         1

same rights as white Americans. They could not eat in some

_____ . Many African Americans could not _____ .
        2   3

_____ , helped change
                        4

laws. He led many peaceful demonstrations. In 1964, he won the

Nobel _____ Prize for his work. Dr. King's dream of equal
              5

_____ is still alive.
       6

black	vote	Martin Luther King, Jr.
rights	Peace	restaurants

LET'S SING

This song is from an old African American church song. It was very popular in the 1960s.

We Shall Overcome

We shall overcome,
We shall overcome,
We shall overcome some day.
Oh, deep in my heart
I do believe
We shall overcome some day.

We'll walk hand in hand,
We'll walk hand in hand,
We'll walk hand in hand some day.
Oh, deep in my heart
I do believe
We shall overcome someday.

We shall live in peace,
We shall live in peace,
We shall live in peace some day.
Oh, deep in my heart
I do believe
We shall overcome some day.

We are not afraid,
We are not afraid,
We are not afraid today.
Oh, deep in my heart
I do believe
We shall overcome some day.

The whole wide world around,
The whole wide world around,
The whole wide world around
 some day.
Oh, deep in my heart
I do believe
We shall overcome some day.

3

BEFORE YOU READ

Talk about this photograph. Guess the answers to the questions below. Write your guesses on the lines.

1. Who are these people? _____

    _____

2. What is the woman holding? _____

    _____

3. What are they celebrating? _____

Now turn the page and read.

    _____

17

Valentine's Day

Valentine's Day is always on February 14. It is not a national holiday. On weekdays, schools are open. Banks are open. People go to work. Life goes on as usual, but there is one difference. People give cards and gifts to friends and people they love. They say, "Be my valentine."

There are many kinds of valentine cards. Some people make cards. Most people buy them. Men and women often give each other romantic cards. These cards say, "I love you." The husband in the picture gave a romantic valentine card to his wife.

Children and friends usually give funny or humorous cards. These cards do not say, "I love you." They are not romantic. Children give cards to their friends at school parties.

Flowers and candy are popular gifts on Valentine's Day. Many people give red roses to people they love. Stores sell chocolates and other candies in heart shapes.

Valentine's Day began long ago. Some people think it started in Roman times. There was a holiday on February 15. On this day, young men chose their sweethearts for the year.

For over a thousand years, Valentine's Day was a religious holiday for Christians. Christians remembered Saint Valentine, a kind priest. He died on February 14, 270. Then in the 1300s, February 14 became a special day for love. People gave cards to their sweethearts. They wrote poems on the cards. They drew pictures of hearts too. Valentine cards became more and more beautiful. There is a picture of a valentine card on page 23.

Today Valentine's Day is not a religious holiday. It is a day for love and friendship. It is also a day for big business. Americans spend millions of dollars on cards and gifts every Valentine's Day. But money cannot buy love and friendship!

UNDERSTANDING NEW WORDS

Take turns reading these sentences with a partner. Does **a** or **b** have the same meaning as the sentence? Decide with your partner. Circle the letter **a** or **b**.

1. Men and women often give each other **romantic** cards. These cards say, "I love you."
   - **a.** People in love give romantic cards.
   - **b.** Friends give each other romantic cards.

2. Flowers and candy are **popular** gifts on Valentine's Day.
   - **a.** Many people give flowers and candy on Valentine's Day.
   - **b.** Not many people give flowers and candy on Valentine's Day.

3. In Roman times, there was a holiday on February 15. On this day, young men chose their **sweethearts** for the year.
   - **a.** On February 15, young men chose their friends for the year.
   - **b.** On February 15, young men chose their girlfriends for the year.

4. Children and friends usually give **humorous** cards.
   - **a.** Children and friends give cards to make people laugh.
   - **b.** Children and friends give cards to make people cry.

UNDERSTANDING WHAT YOU READ

When Is the Holiday?

Fill in the year. Then write the dates for February. Circle Valentine's Day.

February 19 ____

Sun.	Mon.	Tues.	Wed.	Thurs.	Fri.	Sat.

Correct the Sentences

Take turns reading these sentences with a partner. One word in each sentence is wrong. Correct each sentence together. Write the new sentence on the line below.

1. Valentine's Day is always on March 14.

   Valentine's Day is always on February 14.

2. Children and friends usually give each other romantic cards on Valentine's Day.

   _____

   _____

3. Children give flowers to their friends at school parties.

   _____

4. Many people give white roses to people they love.

   _____

5. On February 15 in Roman times, young women chose their sweethearts for the year.

   _____

   _____

6. Americans spend hundreds of dollars on valentine cards and gifts each year.

   _____

   _____

True or False?

Take turns reading these sentences with a partner. Is each sentence true or false? Decide with your partner. Put an *X* under TRUE or FALSE.

		TRUE	FALSE
1.	Flowers and candy are popular Valentine gifts.	X	
2.	The date of Valentine's Day changes every year.		
3.	Valentine's Day is a day for love, friendship, and big business.		
4.	Valentine's Day is a religious holiday in the United States.		
5.	Valentine's Day is for children only.		

BEFORE YOU CONTINUE

- Look at your guesses on page 17. Were you right?
- Now fill in Valentine's Day on the Holiday Chart on page 153.

TALK ABOUT IT

What is important in a girlfriend or boyfriend? Interview a partner about these 10 qualities. Circle 1, 2, 3, or 4 for each.

Partner's Name: _____

QUALITY	1 Very Important	2 Important	3 Not Very Important	4 Not Important
looks	1	2	3	4
age	1	2	3	4
nationality	1	2	3	4
religion	1	2	3	4
income	1	2	3	4
education	1	2	3	4
honesty	1	2	3	4
sense of humor	1	2	3	4
kindness	1	2	3	4
romance	1	2	3	4

Which three qualities are the most important? Ask your partner. Write your partner's answers here. Then share the answers with the class.

1. _____

2. _____

3. _____

WRITE

On Valentine's Day, some people make cards for their friends and sweethearts. Others buy cards like the one below. Some people put messages in the newspaper for their friends and sweethearts to read.

Look at this valentine card and these valentine messages from the newspaper.

KENNY
To my Sweetheart and love of my life. Forever we'll be together.   *Yours Always.*

LOVE

Kristine ♥ ♥ ♥ ♥
Happy Valentine's Day to the one I love with all my heart and soul. You make me the luckiest man in the world.
Love Steven XXX000

M.G.
be my Valentine ♥
I love you!
I will always love you!!
Always, Forever!!!
Maria

MARY ANN
Happy Valentine's Day!
Happy Anniversary!
8 is great, but 9 will be even better.
Love Joe

LOUIE & GLORIA AVILA
To the special Husband and Daughter in my life.   Love always, Aida

Now write a valentine greeting for someone you love.

_____

_____

_____

LET'S SING

There are many American love songs. People first sang this love song in 1910. It was very popular. People sing this song today too.

Let Me Call You Sweetheart

Let me call you sweetheart,
I'm in love with you.
Let me hear you whisper,
That you love me too.
Keep the love-light glowing,
In your eyes so true.
Let me call you sweetheart,
I'm in love with you.

Repeat.

BEFORE YOU READ

Talk about these photographs. Guess the answers to the
questions below. Write your guesses on the lines.

1. How old are these houses? _____

_____

2. Were the people in the houses rich or poor? _____

_____

3. Who lived in these houses? _____

_____

*Now turn the
page and read.*

Presidents' Day

The third Monday in February is Presidents' Day. On this day, Americans remember two important Presidents, George Washington and Abraham Lincoln.

George Washington was born on February 22, 1732, in Virginia. He came from a rich family. His family home, Mount Vernon, is the house in the top picture. During the Revolutionary War (1775–1783), Washington helped the 13 colonies become free from England. After the war, Washington helped write the Constitution, the law for the new country.

In 1789, George Washington became the first President of the United States. He was President for eight years. In 1797, he retired. He went back to Mount Vernon and died there in 1799.

Abraham Lincoln was born in Kentucky on February 12, 1809. His family was poor. Lincoln did not go to school very often, but he learned to read and write. When he was 22, his family moved to Illinois. Here he worked and lived in a store. This store is in the bottom picture. Lincoln became a lawyer and later a congressman. In 1861, he became the sixteenth President.

Lincoln was President for four very difficult years. The northern states fought the southern states in the Civil War. The South wanted slavery. The North did not believe in owning people. Lincoln freed many slaves in 1864. The Civil War ended on April 9, 1865. Five days later, a man from the South assassinated Lincoln. He shot and killed Lincoln in Washington, D.C.

Americans honor these two Presidents in many ways. Some U.S. money has pictures of Washington or Lincoln on it. Many cities, schools, and streets have the names Washington or Lincoln. George Washington is the only President with a state named after him! Many people visit the Washington Monument and the Lincoln Memorial in Washington, D.C. There is a picture of the Lincoln Memorial on page 28. People also visit Mount Vernon in Virginia and Lincoln's homes in Illinois. In 1971, Presidents' Day became a national holiday.

UNDERSTANDING NEW WORDS

Take turns reading these sentences with a partner. Does **a, b,** or **c** mean the same as the underlined word? Decide with your partner. Circle **a, b,** or **c**.

1. George Washington was President for eight years. In 1797, he <u>retired</u>.
   - a. returned to work
   - (b.) stopped working
   - c. looked for a new job

2. George Washington <u>went back to</u> Mount Vernon and died there in 1799.
   - a. left
   - b. sold
   - c. returned to

3. The northern states <u>fought</u> the southern states in the Civil War.
   - a. were at war with
   - b. bought
   - c. liked

4. The South wanted <u>slavery</u>. The North did not believe in it.
   - a. to shoot people
   - b. to hire people
   - c. to own people

5. Five days after the Civil War ended, a man from the South <u>assassinated</u> Lincoln in Washington, D.C.
   - a. visited
   - b. killed
   - c. injured

6. George Washington is the only President with a state <u>named after</u> him.
   - a. with his name
   - b. with his picture
   - c. without a name

UNDERSTANDING WHAT YOU READ

When Is the Holiday?

Fill in the year. Then write the dates for February. Circle Presidents' Day.

February 19 ____

Sun.	Mon.	Tues.	Wed.	Thurs.	Fri.	Sat.

The Lincoln Memorial in Washington, D.C.

Washington or Lincoln?

Take turns reading these sentences with a partner. Is each sentence about George Washington or about Abraham Lincoln? Decide with your partner. Put an X under WASHINGTON or LINCOLN.

	WASHINGTON	LINCOLN
1. His birthday is February 22.	**X**	
2. He was the sixteenth President.		
3. He freed the slaves.		
4. A man assassinated him.		
5. He lived at Mount Vernon.		
6. His birthday is February 12.		
7. He fought in the Revolutionary War.		
8. He was a lawyer.		
9. He was President for eight years.		
10. He was the first President of the United States.		

Understanding Time Order

Read these sentences with a partner. Decide together what happened first, second, third, and so on. Put the sentences in order from 1 to 8.

_____Lincoln freed many slaves.

___1___Washington helped the colonies during the Revolutionary War.

_____Washington died at Mount Vernon.

_____Presidents' Day became a national holiday.

_____Washington became the first President.

_____A man assassinated Lincoln in Washington, D.C.

_____Lincoln was born in Kentucky.

_____Lincoln became a lawyer.

BEFORE YOU CONTINUE

- Look at your guesses on page 25. Were you right?
- Now fill in Presidents' Day on the Holiday Chart on page 153.

TALK ABOUT IT

This chart is about the two buildings on page 25. Your chart is missing the information about the Lincoln-Berry store in New Salem Village. Ask your partner questions and write the missing information in the chart. *Do not* look at your partner's book.

	Mount Vernon	Lincoln-Berry Store
What President lived here?	George Washington	
When did the President live here?	1754–1788 1797–1799	
Where is this building?	Alexandria, Virginia	
When was it built?	1735	
How many people visit each year?	about 1,000,000	
What days is it open?	every day	
What time is it open?	summer hours: 9:00 A.M.–5:00 P.M.	
How much does it cost to visit?	ages 12–62 $5.00	
Is there a museum?	yes	
Is there a gift shop?	yes	
Is there a restaurant?	yes	

TALK ABOUT IT

This chart is about the two buildings on page 25. Your chart is missing the information about Mount Vernon. Ask your partner questions and write the missing information in the chart. *Do not* look at your partner's book.

	Mount Vernon	Lincoln-Berry Store
What President lived here?		Abraham Lincoln
When did the President live here?		1833–1837
Where is this building?		Petersburg, Illinois
When was it built?		1831
How many people visit each year?		about 570,000
What days is it open?		every day except New Year's, Thanksgiving, and Christmas
What time is it open?		summer hours: 9:00 A.M. to 5:00 P.M.
How much does it cost to visit?		free
Is there a museum?		yes
Is there a gift shop?		yes
Is there a restaurant?		yes

WRITE

Write three sentences about George Washington. Look back at the story if you need help.

1. _____

2. _____

3. _____

Write three sentences about Abraham Lincoln. Look back at the story if you need help.

1. _____

2. _____

3. _____

WRITE

Now write five sentences about another political leader. Choose a leader from your native country or from the United States. Then share your sentences with the class.

1. _____

2. _____

3. _____

4. _____

5. _____

BEFORE YOU READ

Talk about this photograph. Guess the answers to the questions below. Write your guesses on the lines.

1. Who are these people? _____

_____

2. What are they doing? _____

_____

Now turn the page and read.

St. Patrick's Day

March 17 is St. Patrick's Day. It is a day to remember the Irish people in the United States and Ireland. Ireland is a country with a lot of green grass and shamrocks. Shamrocks are small plants with three leaves. There is a lot of green in Ireland, so green is Ireland's national color.

People often wear green clothes on St. Patrick's Day. There are parades like the one in the picture. Many people go to parties. They sing, dance, and eat Irish food. Some people even drink green beer. In Chicago, the Chicago River is dyed green!

St. Patrick was a priest in Ireland many years ago. He taught the Irish people about God. There are many stories about St. Patrick. One story says there are no snakes in Ireland because St. Patrick sent them away. St. Patrick died on March 17 in the year 461.

Beginning in 1845, many Irish people moved to the United States. They came because there wasn't enough food to eat in Ireland. St. Patrick's Day celebrations helped the Irish remember their country, their music, and their families.

Today's immigrants to the United States also bring celebrations with them. Chinese people celebrate Chinese New Year in January or February. On Chinese New Year, some Chinese people dress like animals and march in parades. They have parties and eat Chinese food.

Mexican people remember May 5, 1862, on *Cinco de mayo*. There was a famous battle on that day. Every year on May 5, Mexicans in Mexico and the United States celebrate with parades and parties.

Many Americans say, "Everyone is Irish on St. Patrick's Day." In the future, they may say, "Everyone is Chinese on Chinese New Year" and "Everyone is Mexican on *Cinco de mayo*."

UNDERSTANDING NEW WORDS

Take turns reading these sentences with a partner. Does **a** or **b** mean the same as the underlined word? Decide with your partner. Circle **a** or **b**.

1. On St. Patrick's Day in Chicago, the Chicago River is <u>dyed</u> green.
   - **(a.)** colored
   - **b.** painted

2. Today's <u>immigrants</u> to the United States also bring celebrations with them.
   - **a.** newcomers
   - **b.** visitors

3. On Chinese New Year, some Chinese people dress like animals and <u>march</u> in parades.
   - **a.** walk together
   - **b.** drive together

4. In Mexico, there was a famous <u>battle</u> on May 5, 1862.
   - **a.** party
   - **b.** fight in a war

UNDERSTANDING WHAT YOU READ

When Is the Holiday?

Fill in the year. Then write the dates for March. Circle St. Patrick's Day.

March 19 ____

Sun.	Mon.	Tues.	Wed.	Thurs.	Fri.	Sat.

Correct the Sentences

Take turns reading these sentences with a partner. One word in each sentence is wrong. Correct each sentence together. Write the new sentence on the line below.

1. Red is Ireland's national color.

   Green is Ireland's national color.

2. On St. Patrick's Day, many people eat Chinese food.

   _____

3. There are no dogs in Ireland because St. Patrick sent them away.

   _____

4. St. Patrick's Day celebrations helped the Irish forget their country, their music, and their families.

   _____

   _____

5. Chinese people celebrate Chinese New Year in January or March.

   _____

6. On *Cinco de mayo,* many people eat Irish food.

   _____

7. Today's visitors to the United States bring celebrations with them.

   _____

   _____

Understanding Sentences with Because

Take turns reading these sentences with a partner. Decide together how to finish each sentence. Cross out the letter of the answer. Then write the letter on the line.

1. Green is Ireland's national color __d__

2. People wear green on St. Patrick's Day _____

3. One story says there are no snakes in Ireland _____

4. Many Irish people moved to the United States _____

5. Chinese people have parades in January or February _____

6. Mexican people celebrate *Cinco de mayo* _____

a. because it is their New Year.

b. because St. Patrick sent them away.

c. because it is the national color of Ireland.

d. because there is a lot of green grass in Ireland.

e. because there was a famous battle on that day.

f. because there was no food to eat in Ireland.

BEFORE YOU CONTINUE

- Look at your guesses on page 35. Were you right?
- Now fill in St. Patrick's Day on the Holiday Chart on page 153.

TALK ABOUT IT

Interview a partner about a special day in his or her native country. Ask these questions and write the answers in the chart. Then share the answers with the class.

1. What is your native country?
2. What is the name of the special day?
3. When do people celebrate this day?
4. Why is this an important day?
5. What do people do on this day?
6. What food do people eat?
7. What songs do people sing?
8. What clothes do people wear?

Partner's Name: _____

1. Country	
2. Name of day	
3. Date	
4. Reason it is important	
5. Activities	
6. Food	
7. Songs	
8. Clothes	

WRITE

Read the story and write in the missing words. Look at the words in the box below the story if you need help.

St. Patrick's Day is ___*always*___ March 17. People wear
₁

_____ in honor of Ireland's national color. People celebrate
₂

with _____ , parties, music, and dancing.
₃

_____ bring many of their celebrations to the United
₄

States with them. *Cinco de mayo* and Chinese New Year are two

holidays immigrants _____ in the U.S. People from all
₅

countries like _____!
₆

green	Immigrants	always
celebrate	parades	parties

LET'S SING

There are many Irish songs. People like to sing them on St. Patrick's Day. Here is a popular Irish song. It is a lullaby, a song parents sing to their young children. Many parents sing lullabies to their children when they go to sleep.

Too-Ra-Loo-Ra-Loo-Ral

Over in Killarney, many years ago,
My mother sang a song to me,
In tones so sweet and low.

Just a simple little ditty
In her dear old Irish way,
And I'd give the world if I could hear
Her sing this song today.

Too-ra-loo-ra-loo-ral,
Too-ra-loo-ra-li,
Too-ra-loo-ra-loo-ral,
Hush, now, don't you cry.

Too-ra-loo-ra-loo-ral,
Too-ra-loo-ra-li,
Too-ra-loo-ra-loo-ral,
That's an Irish lullaby.

BEFORE YOU READ

Talk about this photograph. Guess the answers to the questions
below. Write your guesses on the lines.

1. Where are these people? _____

   _____

2. What is the father doing? _____

   _____

3. Why are the children laughing? _____

   _____

Now turn the
page and read.

April Fools' Day

The Watson family is eating breakfast. They are having cereal and orange juice. Mr. Watson is waiting for the coffee.

FATHER: Is the coffee ready yet?

MOTHER: Yes. Would you like a cup?

FATHER: Yes, please.

Mrs. Watson pours the coffee. Mr. Watson puts milk and sugar into his cup. The children watch as their father drinks the coffee.

FATHER: Yuk! This is terrible! It tastes salty!

CHILDREN: April Fool!

The children start to laugh. Last night, Mrs. Watson and the children put salt in the sugar jar.

April 1 is April Fools' Day. Many people like to play jokes or tricks on this day. The jokes are for fun only. They are not harmful or mean. The Watson children tricked their father when they put salt in the sugar jar.

Sometimes you can hear April Fools' Day jokes on the radio or television. Newspapers often have silly stories on April 1 too. Some silly headlines are on the next page. If you believe the jokes on the radio, TV, or in the newspaper, you are an "April Fool."

Nobody knows where or when April Fools' Day started. Some people believe it started in France in the 1500s. Some people think it started long ago in Italy. Other people believe it started in India.

Some people think April Fools' Day started because of the spring weather. In the spring, the weather changes every day. The spring weather tricks people. But people in Mexico celebrate Fools' Day in winter, on December 28.

It doesn't matter where or when April Fools' Day began. Americans like it because they can play jokes on friends and relatives.

```
THE DAILY JOURNAL                    April 1, 2000

PRESIDENT PAINTS WHITE HOUSE BLACK
═══════════════════════    ═══════════════════════
───────────────────────    ───────────────────────
───────────────────────    ───────────────────────
───────────────────────    ───────────────────────
───────────────────────    ───────────────────────

  DOG DRIVES CAR          MOON BECOMES
   TO HOSPITAL            51ST STATE
```

UNDERSTANDING NEW WORDS

Take turns reading these sentences with a partner. Does **a** or **b** mean the same as the underlined word? Decide with your partner. Circle **a** or **b.**

1. April Fool jokes are for fun only. They are not harmful or <u>mean</u>.
    - **a.** kind
    - **(b.)** bad

2. The Watson children <u>tricked</u> their father when they put salt in the sugar jar.
    - **a.** hurt
    - **b.** fooled

3. Newspapers often have <u>silly</u> stories on April 1.
    - **a.** serious
    - **b.** funny

4. It <u>doesn't matter</u> where or when April Fools' Day began.
    - **a.** isn't very important
    - **b.** is very important

5. Americans like April Fools' Day because they can play jokes on friends and <u>relatives</u>.
    - **a.** neighbors
    - **b.** family

UNDERSTANDING WHAT YOU READ

When Is the Holiday?

Fill in the year. Then write the dates for April. Circle April Fools' Day.

April 19 _____

Sun.	Mon.	Tues.	Wed.	Thurs.	Fri.	Sat.

Understanding Questions with When

Take turns reading these questions with a partner. Decide together how to answer each question. Write the answer on the line below.

1. When did the children put salt in the sugar jar?

   _____

2. When is April Fools' Day?

   _____

3. When did April Fools' Day start?

   _____

4. When did April Fools' Day start in France?

   _____

5. When do people in Mexico celebrate Fools' Day?

   _____

BEFORE YOU CONTINUE

- Look at your guesses on page 43. Were you right?
- Now fill in April Fools' Day on the Holiday Chart on page 153.

 ## TALK ABOUT IT

Work with a small group or a partner. Talk about each joke. Is it fun or mean? Circle FUN or MEAN. Then share your answers with the class.

1. Some students put balloons in their teacher's car.   FUN   MEAN

2. A mother wakes up her children at midnight and tells them it is time for school.   FUN   MEAN

3. A mother gives her family hamburgers for breakfast.   FUN   MEAN

4. You invite friends to your house for dinner. You are not home.   FUN   MEAN

5. A boy puts a plastic spider in his sister's bed.   FUN   MEAN

6. Some children put pennies in their father's shoes.   FUN   MEAN

WRITE

Work with a small group or a partner. Plan an April Fools' Day joke for a teacher, a parent or spouse, and a best friend. Write your jokes on the lines. Then share them with the class.

A teacher: _____

_____

_____

A parent or spouse: _____

_____

_____

A best friend: _____

_____

_____

BEFORE YOU READ

Talk about this photograph. Guess the answers to the questions below. Write your guesses on the lines.

1. Where are these children? _____

   _____

2. What is the girl holding? _____

   _____

3. What season is it? _____

   _____

Now turn the page and read.

Easter

Easter is on a different Sunday each year. But it is always in March or April. Easter is not a national holiday. It is a religious holiday for Christians. For many people, Easter celebrates the beginning of spring.

The English word *Easter* comes from the Old English word *Eastre*. Eastre was the name of the goddess of spring and light. In the spring, flowers bloom and trees become green. The earth wears "new clothes." Many people wear new clothes on Easter Sunday too.

Eggs and rabbits are signs of spring and new life. American children believe in an imaginary rabbit, the Easter bunny. The night before Easter, the Easter bunny visits many homes. He brings children Easter baskets with eggs and candy. Some Easter eggs are hard-boiled eggs in different colors. Other Easter eggs are chocolate. The Easter bunny hides eggs in the house or outside in the yard. On Easter morning, children look for eggs from the Easter bunny. The girl in the picture is holding an Easter egg. She found it in the grass.

For millions of Christians, Easter is a religious holiday. Two days before Easter is Good Friday. Christians believe Jesus Christ died on this day. Many schools and businesses close on Good Friday. Christians also believe Jesus rose from the dead on Easter Sunday. Easter is a very joyful holiday for Christians. Many go to church on Good Friday and on Easter.

There is also an important Jewish holiday in the spring. For eight days, Jewish people celebrate Passover. Passover and Easter are often in the same month.

On Easter Sunday, families often come together for a dinner of ham or lamb with fresh spring vegetables. Dessert is often cake in the shape of a lamb or rabbit. And there is plenty of candy from the Easter bunny!

UNDERSTANDING NEW WORDS

Take turns reading these sentences with a partner. Does **a** or **b** have the same meaning as the sentence? Decide with your partner. Circle **a** or **b.**

1. In the spring, flowers **bloom,** and trees become green.
   - **(a.)** Flowers grow in the spring.
   - **b.** Flowers die in the spring.

2. Eggs and rabbits are **signs** of spring and new life.
   - **a.** Eggs and rabbits mean winter is coming.
   - **b.** Eggs and rabbits mean spring is here.

3. American children believe in an **imaginary** rabbit.
   - **a.** American children believe in a real rabbit.
   - **b.** American children believe in a rabbit. It is not real.

4. Easter dessert is often cake in the **shape** of a lamb or rabbit.
   - **a.** Easter cakes look like lambs or rabbits.
   - **b.** Lambs or rabbits eat the Easter cakes.

5. There is **plenty** of candy from the Easter bunny.
   - **a.** The Easter bunny brings a lot of candy for the children.
   - **b.** The Easter bunny brings a little candy for the children.

UNDERSTANDING WHAT YOU READ

When Is the Holiday?

Fill in the year. Then write the dates for March and April. Circle Easter.

March 19 ____

Sun.	Mon.	Tues.	Wed.	Thurs.	Fri.	Sat.

April 19 ____

Sun.	Mon.	Tues.	Wed.	Thurs.	Fri.	Sat.

Correct the Sentences

Take turns reading these sentences with a partner. One word in each sentence is wrong. Correct each sentence together. Write the new sentence on the line below.

1. Easter is on a different Saturday each year.

   Easter is on a different Sunday each year.

2. The word *Easter* comes from the name of a goddess of spring and dark.

   _____

   _____

3. Many people wash new clothes on Easter Sunday.

   _____

4. The night before Easter, the Easter chicken visits many homes.

   _____

5. On Easter morning, adults look for baskets from the Easter bunny.

   _____

   _____

6. Many schools and churches close on Good Friday.

   _____

7. Easter is a very sad holiday for Christians.

   _____

8. For five days, Jewish people celebrate Passover.

   _____

BEFORE YOU CONTINUE

- Look at your guesses on page 49. Were you right?
- Now fill in Easter on the Holiday Chart on page 153.

TALK ABOUT IT, *Activity 1*

Talk about these things with a partner or a small group. Six things are not related to Easter. One is crossed out. Cross out five more. Then share your answers with the class.

~~snow~~	picnics
flags	the Easter bunny
Christmas carols	hamburgers
rabbits	chocolate rabbits
baskets	electric lights
colored eggs	new clothes
green	lamb cakes
flowers	church

TALK ABOUT IT, *Activity 2*

Colored Easter eggs are popular in many countries. In the United States, stores sell Easter egg–coloring kits. Families often dye, or color, Easter eggs together.

     With a partner or a small group, read these directions for dyeing Easter eggs. Decide together what to do first, second, third, and so on. Put the directions in order from 1 to 9.

_____ Hard-boil the eggs.

_____ Mix water, vinegar, and dye in small cups.

_____ Read the directions on the kit.

__**1**__ Go to the grocery store.

_____ Put the eggs in the small cups with the dye.

_____ Cool the eggs.

_____ Put the eggs in a basket.

_____ Buy eggs and a coloring kit.

_____ Let the eggs dry.

Share your answers with the class. Now you are ready to dye Easter eggs!

WRITE

There are four seasons of the year—winter, spring, summer, and fall. Most people have a favorite season.

A student from Poland wrote this about his favorite season. Read his story.

Winter

Winter is my favorite season. I feel good when it is cold outside. I like to ski and ice-skate. I like to wear wool clothes.

In the winter, hot tea is a good drink. And I like to eat beef stew when it is cold outside.

Now write about your favorite season. Then share your story with the class.

_____

_____ is my favorite season. I feel _____

when it is _____ outside. I like to _____ and

_____ . I like to wear _____ .

In the _____ , _____ is a good drink.

And I like to eat _____ when it is _____

outside.

BEFORE YOU READ

Talk about this photograph. Guess the answers to the questions below. Write your guesses on the lines.

1. What is the woman doing? _____

    _____

2. What is she holding? _____

    _____

3. How does she feel? _____

    _____

Now turn the page and read.

Mother's Day and Father's Day

The second Sunday in May is Mother's Day. Americans remember mothers and grandmothers on this day. People give cards and flowers to their mothers and grandmothers. Sometimes they give other gifts such as scarves or jewelry. The woman in the picture received a scarf from her children. "Happy Mother's Day!" her family tells her. They thank their mother for her hard work and love.

On Mother's Day, families may help their mother with her work. It is her day off.

Anna Jarvis, a woman from West Virginia, first thought of Mother's Day. She started the custom of using flowers to honor mothers. In 1914, President Woodrow Wilson made Mother's Day a national commemorative day.

Americans also have a special day for fathers. Father's Day is the third Sunday in June. On this day, people give gifts to their fathers and grandfathers. Some families go to restaurants on Father's Day. Other families have a nice dinner at home.

A woman from Washington State, Sonora Dodd, first thought of Father's Day. When she was a young girl, her mother died. Her father raised five sons and a daughter by himself. Sonora Dodd wanted to honor her father for his hard work and love. In 1910, she started the first Father's Day in Washington State. Many years later, in 1972, Father's Day became a national commemorative day.

When Anna Jarvis and Sonora Dodd were mothers, most women stayed home. They didn't go to work. They cooked, cleaned, and took care of children. Today families are changing. In most families in the United States, both mothers and fathers go to work. Many men cook, clean, and take care of children. Some fathers stay home and the mothers go to work.

On Mother's Day and Father's Day, people say thank you and "I love you" to their parents.

A family spends Father's Day together.

UNDERSTANDING NEW WORDS

Take turns reading these sentences with a partner. Does **a** or **b** mean the same as the underlined words? Decide with your partner. Circle **a** or **b**.

1. Many mothers have a <u>day off</u> on Mother's Day.
   - **a.** day without work
   - **b.** workday

2. In 1914, President Woodrow Wilson made Mother's Day a <u>national commemorative day.</u>
   - **a.** day for Americans to honor something important
   - **b.** vacation day

3. Sonora Dodd's father <u>raised</u> five sons and a daughter by himself.
   - **a.** took care of
   - **b.** adopted

4. Sonora Dodd's father raised five sons and a daughter <u>by himself.</u>
   - **a.** with help from a friend
   - **b.** alone, without any help

5. Sonora Dodd wanted to <u>honor</u> her father for his hard work and love.
   - **a.** kiss
   - **b.** thank

UNDERSTANDING WHAT YOU READ

When Is the Holiday?

Fill in the year. Then write the dates for May and June. Circle Mother's Day and Father's Day.

May 19 _____

Sun.	Mon.	Tues.	Wed.	Thurs.	Fri.	Sat.

June 19 _____

Sun.	Mon.	Tues.	Wed.	Thurs.	Fri.	Sat.

Correct the Sentences

Take turns reading these sentences with a partner. One word in each sentence is wrong. Correct each sentence together. Write the new sentence on the line below.

1. The second Sunday in March is Mother's Day.

    The second Sunday in May is Mother's Day.

2. People give cards and flowers to their mothers and grandmothers on Father's Day.

_____

_____

3. Many families go to a supermarket for brunch or dinner on Mother's Day.

_____

_____

4. Anna Jarvis, a man from West Virginia, first thought of Mother's Day.

_____

_____

5. Father's Day is the third Monday in June.

_____

6. When Sonora Dodd was a young girl, her father died.

_____

7. Sonora Dodd wanted to honor her father for his easy work and love.

_____

_____

8. The first Father's Day was in 1910 in Washington, D.C.

_____

BEFORE YOU CONTINUE

- Look at your guesses on page 57. Were you right?
- Now fill in Mother's Day and Father's Day on the Holiday Chart on page 154.

 TALK ABOUT IT, *Activity 1*

Work with a partner or a small group. Decide who should do these jobs for a family—the mother, the father, or both the mother and the father. Put an *X* in the answer column you choose. Then share your answers with the class.

JOB	Mother	Father	Both
go to work			
stay home with the children			
go grocery shopping			
fix the car			
cook dinner			
paint the living room			
clean the bathroom			
do the laundry			
pay the bills			
take the children to the doctor			

TALK ABOUT IT, *Activity 2*

With a partner or a small group, look at the gifts pictured below. You have $35.00 to buy gifts for your mother and father. What will you buy? Write the names of the gifts and the prices in the chart.

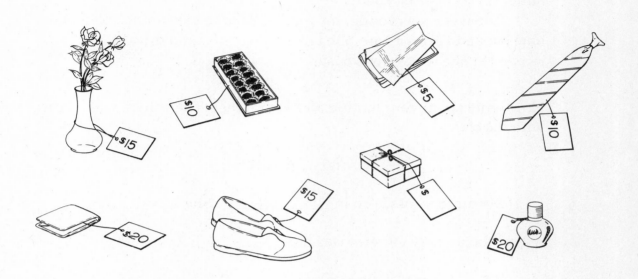

	Gift	Price
Mother		
Father		

TOTAL: $ _____

WRITE

Maria wrote a story about her mother. Read her story.

My Mother

My mother was born in Chicago. She was 17 when she met my father. I was her first child.

When she was young, my mother liked to play tennis. She had blue eyes and brown hair. She taught me to sew and drive. I remember she was always busy.

Now write about your mother and your father. Then share your stories with the class.

My Mother

My mother was born in _____ . She was _____ when she met my father. I was her _____ child.

When she was young, my mother liked to _____ . She had _____ eyes and _____ hair. She taught me to _____ and _____ .

I remember she was always _____ .

My Father

My father was born in _____ . He was _____ when he met my mother. I was his _____ child.

When he was young, my father liked to _____ . He had_____ eyes and _____ hair. He taught me to _____ and _____ . I remember he was always _____ .

BEFORE YOU READ

Talk about this photograph. Guess the answers to the questions below. Write your guesses on the lines.

1. Where are these people? _____

    _____

2. What are they doing? _____

    _____

Now turn the page and read.

Memorial Day

The last Monday in May is Memorial Day. This is a national holiday to remember the dead. Many people visit cemeteries on Memorial Day. They decorate graves with flowers in memory of the dead. In the picture, a child is putting flowers on his grandfather's grave. The grandfather was a soldier in World War II.

The first Memorial Day was many years ago after the Civil War (1861–1865). The northern states fought the southern states. The South wanted slavery, but the North did not believe in owning people. Thousands of soldiers died in the war.

After the war, people wanted to remember the dead. So around 1866, people began to decorate the graves of Civil War soldiers. People called this day Decoration Day. For many years, Decoration Day was on May 30 in most states. Then the name changed from Decoration Day to Memorial Day. In 1971, Memorial Day became a national holiday on the last Monday in May.

Memorial Day had another name after World War I. Some people called it Poppy Day. Poppies are small red flowers. These flowers grew on the battlefields in France. American soldiers, veterans of the war, began to sell poppies for Decoration Day. They gave the money from the poppies to poor children in Europe. Veterans today sell small paper poppies for Memorial Day. The money helps poor and sick veterans.

Americans bury many veterans in Arlington National Cemetery in Virginia. On Memorial Day, the President or Vice President puts flowers on soldiers' tombs to honor all veterans. On page 125 is a picture of the Vice President at Arlington National Cemetery.

Memorial Day is a three-day weekend for most Americans. Some people don't think about the dead on Memorial Day. They think about summer vacations. They go on picnics and enjoy the warm weather. But Memorial Day is a day to remember deceased friends, relatives, and veterans.

UNDERSTANDING NEW WORDS

Take turns reading these sentences with a partner. Does **a** or **b** mean the same as the underlined word? Decide with your partner. Circle **a** or **b**.

1. Many people visit <u>cemeteries</u> on Memorial Day.
    - a.   places to go shopping
    - **(b.)**   places to bury dead people

2. People decorate graves with flowers <u>in memory of</u> the dead.
    - a.   to remember
    - b.   to forget

3. In the Civil War, the South wanted <u>slavery</u>, but the North did not believe in owning people.
    - a.   to buy and sell people
    - b.   to help people

4. Poppies, small red flowers, grew on the <u>battlefields</u> in France.
    - a.   places for soldiers to buy flowers
    - b.   places for soldiers to fight in a war

5. Americans bury many <u>veterans</u> in Arlington National Cemetery in Virginia.
    - a.   soldiers
    - b.   policemen

6. Memorial Day is a day to remember <u>deceased</u> friends, relatives, and veterans.
    - a.   living
    - b.   dead

UNDERSTANDING WHAT YOU READ

When Is the Holiday?

Fill in the year. Then write the dates for May. Circle Memorial Day.

May 19 _____

Sun.	Mon.	Tues.	Wed.	Thurs.	Fri.	Sat.

Correct the Sentences

Take turns reading these sentences with a partner. One word in each sentence is wrong. Correct each sentence together. Then write the new sentence on the line below.

1. The first Monday in May is Memorial Day.

   The last Monday in May is Memorial Day.

2. In the picture, a child is putting money on his grandfather's grave.

   _____

3. The first Memorial Day was many years ago, after the Revolutionary War.

   _____

4. After the Civil War, people wanted to remember the living.

   _____

5. In 1866, people began to decorate the homes of Civil War soldiers.

   _____

6. American veterans from World War I began to sell candy for Decoration Day.

   _____

   _____

7. Veterans today sell poppies for Memorial Day, and the money helps poor and sick students.

   _____

   _____

8. Memorial Day is a two-day weekend for most Americans.

   _____

9. On Memorial Day, people go on picnics and enjoy the cold weather.

   _____

   _____

Understanding Sentences with So

Take turns reading these sentences with a partner. Decide together how to finish each sentence. Cross out the letter of the answer. Then write the letter on the line.

1. Memorial Day is a national holiday to remember the dead,

   __c__

   a. so they called the day Decoration Day.

2. The northern states and the southern states did not believe

   in the same things, _____

   b. so they sold poppies and gave the money to poor children.

3. Many people decorated graves

   with flowers on May 30, _____

   X so many people go to cemeteries on this day.

4. After World War I, veterans wanted to help poor children in

   Europe, _____

   d. so there was a Civil War.

5. Memorial Day is always on a

   Monday, _____

   e. so most people have a three-day weekend.

BEFORE YOU CONTINUE

- Look at your guesses on page 65. Were you right?
- Now fill in Memorial Day on the Holiday Chart on page 154.

TALK ABOUT IT, *Activity 1*

Talk about these things with a partner or a small group. Six things are not related to Memorial Day. One is crossed out. Cross out five more. Then share your answers with the class.

veterans	presents
~~greeting cards~~	popcorn
war	flowers
candy	cemeteries
Civil War	radio
slavery	World War I
picnics	three-day weekend
poppies	turkey

TALK ABOUT IT, *Activity 2*

Talk with a partner or a small group about these things to do on Memorial Day weekend. Choose things to do each day and write them in the chart. Then share your answers with the class.

go fishing	go to a movie	plant vegetables in the garden
have a picnic	go shopping	clean the house
go to the zoo	cut the grass	go for a drive
go to a Memorial Day parade	go to church or temple	have friends over for dinner
visit the cemetery	watch television	visit friends or family

Other things to do: _____

_____

	Saturday	Sunday	Monday
Morning			
Afternoon			
Evening			

WRITE

Memorial Day is a day to remember deceased friends, relatives, and veterans. A student from Japan wrote about someone she remembers. Read her story.

My Grandmother

I remember my grandmother very well. She was very kind to me when I was a child. She played games with me and told me stories. We went for long walks together. She taught me to sew, and we made doll clothes. I still have the doll clothes. When I see them, I think about my grandmother.

Now write about someone you remember.

_____

_____

_____

_____

_____

_____

_____

_____

LET'S SING

This is a famous Civil War song. People worried about their sons and relatives in the war. They wanted them to come home safely. "Johnny" is a Civil War soldier.

When Johnny Comes Marching Home

When Johnny comes marching home again,
Hurrah! Hurrah!
We'll give him a hearty welcome then,
Hurrah! Hurrah!

The men will cheer and the boys will shout,
The ladies they will all turn out,
And we'll all feel glad
When Johnny comes marching home.

Repeat.

BEFORE YOU READ

Talk about this photograph. Guess the answers to the questions below. Write your guesses on the lines.

1. What is the woman doing? _____

   _____

2. What day is this? _____

   _____

Now turn the page and read.

75

Flag Day

On June 14, 1777, the United States adopted its first flag. Today Americans honor the U.S. flag each year on June 14. Flag Day is a national commemorative day. It is not a holiday from work. Many people fly the flag outside their homes and businesses on this day. In the picture, a woman is putting up a flag.

The American flag has different names. One name is "The Red, White, and Blue." This name is for the colors of the flag. Another name is "The Stars and Stripes." This name is for the 50 stars and 13 stripes.

The flag did not always have 50 stars and 13 stripes. In 1777, the original flag had 13 stars and 13 stripes for the 13 colonies. The 13 colonies became the first 13 states. Then more states joined the United States. In 1794, the flag had 15 stars and 15 stripes. Then more states joined. This created a problem for the flag makers. The flag was getting too big! So in 1818, Congress decided to have only 13 stripes on the flag. They decided to add one star for each new state.

The number of stars changed many times. From 1912 to 1959, there were 48 stars. Then in 1959, Alaska and Hawaii joined the United States. So now there are 50 stars on the flag.

The national anthem of the United States is about the flag. It is "The Star-Spangled Banner." Francis Scott Key wrote this song in 1814. People sing it at baseball games and other public events.

There are many rules about how to fly the flag. But the rules don't say anything about the size of the flag. In 1923, a store in Detroit, Michigan, made a huge U.S. flag. It was 270 feet wide and 90 feet high (about 82 meters wide and 27 meters high). Wow!

UNDERSTANDING NEW WORDS

Take turns reading these sentences with a partner. Does **a** or **b** mean the same as the underlined word? Decide with your partner. Circle **a** or **b**.

1. On June 14, 1777, the United States <u>adopted</u> its first flag.
   - **(a.)** chose
   - **b.** changed

2. Flag Day is a national <u>commemorative day</u>. It is not a holiday from work.
   - **a.** day for Americans to remember something important
   - **b.** vacation day

3. In 1777, the <u>original</u> flag had 13 stars and 13 stripes for the 13 colonies.
   - **a.** first
   - **b.** old

4. More states <u>joined</u> the United States.
   - **a.** left
   - **b.** became part of

5. This <u>created</u> a problem for the flag makers.
   - **a.** made
   - **b.** ended

6. The national <u>anthem</u> of the United States is about the flag.
   - **a.** song
   - **b.** color

7. In 1923, a store in Detroit, Michigan, made a <u>huge</u> U.S. flag.
   - **a.** very big
   - **b.** very small

UNDERSTANDING WHAT YOU READ

When Is the Holiday?

Fill in the year. Then write the dates for June. Circle Flag Day.

June 19 __

Sun.	Mon.	Tues.	Wed.	Thurs.	Fri.	Sat.

Understanding Sentences with Because

Take turns reading these sentences with a partner. Decide together how to finish each sentence. Cross out the letter of the answer. Then write the letter on the line.

1. The flag changed many times

   __c__

2. The original flag had 13 stars

   and 13 stripes _____

3. One name for the flag is "The

   Red, White, and Blue" _____

4. Many people fly the flag on June

   14 _____

5. Today the U.S. flag has 50 stars

   _____

a. because there are 50 states.

b. because there were 13 colonies.

~~c.~~ because new states joined the United States.

d. because those are the colors of the flag.

e. because they want to honor the flag.

Understanding Time Order

Take turns reading these sentences with a partner. Decide together what happened first, second, third, and so on. Put the sentences in order from 1 to 6.

_____ The flag has 50 stars.

_____ Francis Scott Key wrote "The Star-Spangled Banner."

_____ A store in Detroit made a huge flag.

___1___ The United States adopted its first flag.

_____ Alaska joined the United States.

_____ The flag had 15 stars and 15 stripes.

BEFORE YOU CONTINUE

- Look at your guesses on page 75. Were you right?
- Now fill in Flag Day on the Holiday Chart on page 154.

TALK ABOUT IT

Interview a partner about the flag in his or her native country. Write the answers in the chart below. Then share the answers with the class.

1. What is your native country?

2. What are the colors of its flag?

3. Is there a day to honor the flag in your native country? When?

4. Does your country have a song about its flag? What is the name of the song?

5. What do people in your native country do when they see the flag?

Partner's Name: _____

1. Country	
2. Colors	
3. Day to honor flag	
4. Song	
5. Activities	

WRITE

Read the story and write in the missing words. Look at the words in the box below the story if you need help.

In 1777, the United States *adopted* its first flag. It had
1

13 stars and 13 stripes for the _____ 13 colonies. Over the
2

years, the flag changed. More and more states _____ the
3

United States. Now there are 50 states. The flag has one _____
4

for each state.

The national _____ is about the flag. People
5

_____ ''The Star-Spangled Banner'' at public events.
6

| sing | joined | adopted |
| star | anthem | original |

LET'S SING

There are many songs about the U.S. flag. "The Star-Spangled Banner" is on page 90. Here is another famous song about the flag.

You're a Grand Old Flag

You're a grand old flag,
You're a high flying flag,
And forever in peace may you wave.
You're the emblem of the land I love,
The home of the free and the brave.

Every heart beats true
For the red, white, and blue
Where there's never a boast or brag.
But should old acquaintance be forgot,
Keep your eye on the grand old flag.

Repeat.

BEFORE YOU READ

Talk about this photograph. Guess the answers to the questions below. Write your guesses on the lines.

1. Where are these people? _____

_____

2. What are they doing? _____

_____

3. What day is it? _____

Now turn the page and read.

_____

Independence Day

July 4 is Independence Day. Another name for Independence Day is the Fourth of July. On this day, Americans remember the first Independence Day on July 4, 1776.

The Revolutionary War began in 1775. The 13 colonies were angry with England. They were tired of paying taxes to King George. They wanted freedom to make laws. So in 1776, leaders from the 13 colonies met in Philadelphia, Pennsylvania. They talked about freedom from England. Thomas Jefferson wrote a paper. The paper, the Declaration of Independence, said the colonies were "free and independent states." The leaders signed it on July 4, 1776.

People in the 13 colonies were very happy about the Declaration of Independence. They made a lot of noise with bells, drums, and guns. People today like to make noise on Independence Day too.

The Fourth of July is a national holiday. Government offices, banks, and schools close. Most people don't go to work. Families and friends get together outside for picnics and cookouts. In the picture, some friends are cooking hamburgers on the grill. An American flag is flying in their backyard. Many Americans fly the flag outside their homes or businesses on July 4.

People also go to Fourth of July parades and listen to patriotic music. In the evening when it gets dark, people watch beautiful fireworks. In most states, people cannot buy fireworks because they are dangerous. People can get hurt. So city governments usually have safe fireworks for everyone to enjoy.

Independence Day isn't only a day for cookouts, noise, and fireworks. It is also a day to think about freedom. The Declaration of Independence says everyone has the right to life, liberty, and the pursuit of happiness. The Declaration of Independence is more than 200 years old, but its ideas are important today.

UNDERSTANDING NEW WORDS

Take turns reading these sentences with a partner. Does **a, b,** or **c** have the same meaning as the sentence? Decide with your partner. Circle **a, b,** or **c.**

1. The 13 colonies were **tired of** paying taxes to King George.
   - a. They didn't want to pay more taxes.
   - b. They wanted to pay more taxes.
   - c. They wanted a new king.

2. In the picture, some friends are cooking hamburgers on a **grill.**
   - a. They are cooking on a stove.
   - b. They are cooking in a microwave oven.
   - c. They are cooking over a fire.

3. On the Fourth of July, families and friends get together outside for picnics and **cookouts.**
   - a. They order food from restaurants.
   - b. They cook food on stoves outside.
   - c. They cook food on grills outside.

4. People go to parades and listen to **patriotic music** on the Fourth of July.
   - a. People listen to rock music.
   - b. People listen to piano music.
   - c. People listen to music about the United States.

5. The Declaration of Independence says everyone has the right to life, **liberty**, and the pursuit of happiness.
   - a. Only men have the right to freedom.
   - b. Everyone has the right to freedom.
   - c. Only women have the right to freedom.

UNDERSTANDING WHAT YOU READ

When Is the Holiday?

Fill in the year. Then write the dates for July. Circle Independence Day.

July 19 ____

Sun.	Mon.	Tues.	Wed.	Thurs.	Fri.	Sat.

True or False?

Take turns reading these sentences with a partner. Is each sentence true or false? Decide with your partner. Put an X under TRUE or FALSE.

		TRUE	FALSE
1.	The first U.S. Independence Day was in 1775.	____	__X__
2.	The 13 colonies wanted freedom from England.	____	____
3.	The people in the 13 colonies were very sad about the Declaration of Independence.	____	____
4.	Independence Day is a quiet day.	____	____
5.	The Fourth of July is a national holiday.	____	____

6. Many people cook outside on the Fourth of July. _____ _____

7. Americans give each other presents on the Fourth of July. _____ _____

8. People watch fireworks on the Fourth of July. _____ _____

9. July 4 is a day to think about freedom. _____ _____

10. The Declaration of Independence is not important today. _____ _____

Understanding Sentences with **So**

Take turns reading these sentences with a partner. Decide together how to finish each sentence. Cross out the letter of the answer. Then write the letter on the line.

1. The Fourth of July is a national holiday, __**b**__

2. The American colonies wanted freedom from England, _____

3. In 1776, people were very happy about the Declaration of Independence, _____

4. The weather in July is warm, _____

5. Fireworks are dangerous, _____

a. so they made a lot of noise with guns, bells, and drums.

b. so most people don't have to go to work.

c. so Thomas Jefferson wrote the Declaration of Independence.

d. so, in most states, people cannot buy them.

e. so people like to have picnics and cookouts on July 4.

BEFORE YOU CONTINUE

- Look at your guesses on page 83. Were you right?
- Now fill in Independence Day (Fourth of July) on the Holiday Chart on page 154.

TALK ABOUT IT, *Activity 1*

The Declaration of Independence says all people have the right to life, liberty, and the pursuit of happiness. Many people come to the United States because they want freedom.

Ask a partner about these eight rights and freedoms. Which are most important to your partner? Write the most important on line 1. Write the least important on line 8.

Partner's Name: _____

the right to vote	1. _____
the freedom to live where you want	2. _____
the freedom of religion	3. _____
the right to own a gun	4. _____
the freedom to travel to other countries	5. _____
the right to education	6. _____
the freedom to choose your job	7. _____
the freedom to read or write what you want	8. _____

Which three rights are most important to your partner? Share these with the class.

TALK ABOUT IT, *Activity 2*

Talk about these things with a partner or a small group. Six things are not related to Independence Day. One is crossed out. Cross out five more. Then share your answers with the class.

flag	fireworks
~~cemetery~~	church
picnic	patriotic music
parade	snow
jail	freedom
England	Canada
turkey	Declaration of Independence
13 colonies	summer

WRITE

Read the story and write in the missing words. Look at the words in the box below the story if you need help.

July 4 is _Independence_ Day in the United States. On this

_____1_____

day, Americans remember their fight for freedom from _____ .

_____2_____

Most people spend the day _____ . People celebrate with

_____3_____

picnics and _____ .Then, in the evening, they watch

_____4_____

beautiful _____ .

_____5_____

The Fourth of July is not only a day for picnics and parades. It is

also a day to celebrate _____ for all.

_____6_____

freedom	outside	parades
England	fireworks	Independence

LET'S SING

The national anthem, or song, of the United States is about the flag. Francis Scott Key wrote this song during the War of 1812.

Today many Americans sing this song on the Fourth of July. They also sing it at baseball games and other public events.

The Star-Spangled Banner

Oh say, can you see,
by the dawn's early light,
What so proudly we hailed
at the twilight's last gleaming?
Whose broad stripes and bright stars,
through the perilous fight,
O'er the ramparts we watched
were so gallantly streaming?
And the rockets' red glare,
the bombs bursting in air,
Gave proof through the night
that our flag was still there.
Oh say, does that star-spangled
banner yet wave
O'er the land of the free
and the home of the brave?

Oh! thus be it ever
when freemen shall stand
Between their loved home
and the war's desolation!
Blest with victory and peace,
may the Heaven-rescued land
Praise the Power that hath made
and preserved us a nation.
Then conquer we must,
when our cause it is just,
And this be our motto:
"In God is our trust."
And the star-spangled banner
in triumph shall wave
O'er the land of the free
and the home of the brave!

Some people think "The Star-Spangled Banner" is hard to sing. They want to change the national anthem of the United States to this song "America the Beautiful."

America the Beautiful

Oh, beautiful for spacious skies,
For amber waves of grain,
For purple mountain majesties
Above the fruited plain!
America! America!
God shed His grace on thee
And crown thy good with
    brotherhood
From sea to shining sea.

Oh, beautiful for pilgrim feet
Whose stern, impassioned stress
A thoroughfare for freedom beat
Across the wilderness.
America! America!
God mend thine every flaw.
Confirm thy soul in self control,
Thy liberty in law.

BEFORE YOU READ

Talk about this photograph. Guess the answers to the questions below. Write your guesses on the lines.

1. Who is this woman? _____

   _____

2. What is she doing? _____

   _____

3. What year is it? _____

   _____

Now turn the page and read.

Labor Day

Life for American workers in the 1800s was not easy. Men and women often worked 12 to 14 hours a day. Even very young children sometimes went to work! Many people worked seven days a week, but they made very little money. They had hard jobs in factories, steel mills, and coal mines. Others built railroads.

Many employers did not treat their workers well. Most workers had no benefits. They had no medical insurance. They had no paid sick days. They didn't have paid vacations. Workers wanted to improve their difficult lives, but they were afraid. They didn't want to lose their jobs. But together they were not so afraid. Workers came together in labor unions.

The first labor union in the United States started in 1869. Through the unions, workers slowly changed their lives. Sometimes workers went on strike. They stopped going to work until their employers made some changes. The woman in the picture is on strike. It is around 1890. She wants better pay and benefits.

Peter J. McGuire was the president of a labor union. He wanted a holiday for workers. He chose September 5, 1882, for the first Labor Day. There was a big parade to honor all the workers in the United States.

In 1894, President Grover Cleveland made Labor Day a national holiday. Labor Day is always the first Monday in September. Most people don't go to work on this day. Many people have a three-day weekend. People enjoy the last days of summer with parades and picnics.

A famous American, Benjamin Franklin, said, "America was built by labor." Labor Day is a day to remember this and to honor all the workers in America.

UNDERSTANDING NEW WORDS

Take turns reading these sentences with a partner. Does **a** or **b** have the same meaning as the sentence? Decide with your partner. Circle **a** or **b**.

1. In the 1800s, most workers had no **benefits.**
   a. Workers received medical insurance, vacation, and sick days.
   (b.) Workers received only their pay.

2. Many employers did not **treat** their workers well.
   a. Many employers gave their workers good benefits.
   b. Many employers did not give their workers any benefits.

3. Workers wanted to **improve** their difficult lives.
   a. Workers were happy with their lives.
   b. Workers wanted better lives.

4. Workers came together in **labor unions.**
   a. Workers with the same problems formed a group.
   b. Workers did not join groups.

5. Sometimes workers went **on strike.**
   a. Sometimes workers refused to work.
   b. Sometimes workers worked 12 hours a day.

UNDERSTANDING WHAT YOU READ

When Is the Holiday?

Fill in the year. Then write the dates for September. Circle Labor Day.

September 19 ____

Sun.	Mon.	Tues.	Wed.	Thurs.	Fri.	Sat.

Correct the Sentences

Take turns reading these sentences with a partner. One word in each sentence is wrong. Correct each sentence together. Write the new sentence on the line below.

1. Life for American employers in the 1800s was not easy.

   Life for American workers in the 1800s was not easy.

2. Many people vacationed seven days a week, but they made very little money.

   _____

   _____

3. Workers didn't want to keep their jobs.

   _____

4. Through the unions, workers quickly changed their lives.

   _____

5. Sometimes employers went on strike for better pay.

   _____

6. Peter J. McGuire was the president of a bank.

   _____

7. Labor Day is always the last Monday in September.

   _____

Understanding Sentences with Because

Take turns reading these sentences with a partner. Decide together how to finish each sentence. Cross out the letter of the answer. Then write the letter on the line.

1. Life for American workers in the 1800s was not easy ___**b**___

    a. because a labor union president wanted a holiday for workers.

2. Workers joined labor unions _____

    ~~b~~. because they worked long hours for little pay.

3. Some employers made changes at work _____

    c. because it is a national holiday, Labor Day.

4. Labor Day started _____

    d. because together they were not afraid of their employers.

5. Many people don't work on the first Monday in September _____

    e. because workers went on strike.

BEFORE YOU CONTINUE

- Look at your guesses on page 91. Were you right?
- Now fill in Labor Day on the Holiday Chart on page 154.

TALK ABOUT IT

In a small group, interview each other about jobs. Talk about the job you have now. If you don't have a job, talk about a job you want to have. Write the answers in the chart. Then share the answers with the class.

	Name:	Name:	Name:
What's your job?			
Where do you work?			
When did you start working there?			
How do you get to work?			
What are your hours?			
How many hours a week do you work?			
Do you have paid vacation days? How many?			
Do you have paid sick days? How many?			
Do you have medical or dental insurance?			
Do you like your job? Why or why not?			

WRITE

A student from Mexico is a teacher's aide. She works in a public school and helps teachers and students in the classroom. Read her story.

I'm a teacher's aide. I work at Lincoln School. I started working there two years ago. I walk to work because the school is near my house. My hours are from 8:30 until 3:15, Monday through Friday. I work five days a week. I don't work in the summer.

My job has good benefits. I have sick days and medical insurance but no vacation time. I really like my job because I like to help students. I hope to be a teacher someday.

Now write about your job. If you don't have a job, write about a job you want to have.

_____

_____

_____

_____

_____

_____

_____

_____

LET'S SING

This song is about a worker in a coal mine. He loads 16 tons of heavy coal every day. He is angry because the work is very hard and the pay is low. He owes a lot of money to the company.

Sixteen Tons

Well now some folks say a man is
    made out of mud,
But a poor man's made out of
    muscle and blood.
Muscle and blood, skin and bone,
A mind that's weak and a back that's
    strong.

You load 16 ton and what do you
    get?
You get another day older and
    deeper in debt.
Saint Peter don't you call me 'cause I
    can't go,
I owe my soul to the company store.

Well I was born one morning when
    the sun didn't shine,
I grabbed my shovel and I went to
    the mine.
I loaded 16 tons of number 9 coal,
The straw boss hollered, "Well
    damn your soul."

You load 16 ton and what do you
    get?
You get another day older and
    deeper in debt.
Saint Peter don't you call me 'cause I
    can't go,
I owe my soul to the company store.

Well I was born one morning in the
    drizzling rain,
Fighting and trouble been my
    middle name.
If you see me coming, you better
    step aside,
A lot of men didn't and a lot of men
    died.

You load 16 ton and what do you
    get?
You get another day older and
    deeper in debt.
Saint Peter don't you call me 'cause I
    can't go,
I owe my soul to the company store.
I owe my soul to the company store.

BEFORE YOU READ

Talk about this picture. Guess the answers to the questions below.
Write your guesses on the lines.

1. Who are these people? _____

_____

2. Where are they? _____

_____

3. What year is it? _____

*Now turn the
page and read.*

Columbus Day

Americans remember Christopher Columbus on Columbus Day. Christopher Columbus was born in 1451 in Italy. He lived in Genoa, a city by the sea. He loved the sea and learned to sail.

In the fifteenth century, Europeans wanted gold and spices from Asia. The trip by land to Asia was very long and difficult. Christopher Columbus wanted to find a faster way to Asia. He wanted to sail west from Spain.

He asked the king and queen of Spain for help. They gave him money for the trip. Columbus bought three ships—the *Niña*, the *Pinta*, and the *Santa María*. In August 1492, Columbus and 83 men left Spain to find Asia.

They sailed for many difficult weeks. On October 12, the men saw land. Columbus thought it was Asia, but he was wrong. The land was the Bahamas, a group of islands. Columbus found a "New World." The picture shows Columbus finding the New World on October 12, 1492. He made four trips to the New World before he died.

Columbus died a poor man. He wasn't famous. But Americans remember him each year on Columbus Day. The first Columbus Day celebration was in New York City in 1792. Now Americans celebrate Columbus Day on the second Monday in October. It is a legal holiday in many states. Most people do not go to work or school. There are Columbus Day parades. Many stores have big sales.

Christopher Columbus was not the first European to come to the New World. About 500 years before Columbus, Leif Ericson sailed from Norway to Canada. He found the New World of North America. In 1964, President Lyndon Johnson named October 9 Leif Ericson Day. So in October, Americans remember two important men, Christopher Columbus and Leif Ericson.

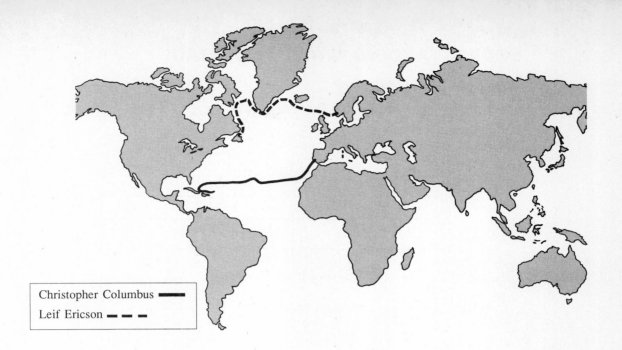

Christopher Columbus ▬▬▬
Leif Ericson ▬ ▬ ▬

UNDERSTANDING NEW WORDS

Take turns reading these pairs of sentences with a partner. Is the meaning of the sentences the same or different? Decide with your partner. Circle SAME or DIFFERENT.

1. Columbus loved the **sea**.
   Columbus loved the water.

   (SAME)   DIFFERENT

2. Columbus learned to **sail**.
   Columbus learned to drive.

   SAME   DIFFERENT

3. Columbus and his men sailed for many **difficult** weeks.
   Columbus and his men sailed for many hard weeks.

   SAME   DIFFERENT

4. The **trip** by land to Asia was very difficult.
   Travel by land to Asia was very difficult.

   SAME   DIFFERENT

UNDERSTANDING WHAT YOU READ

When Is the Holiday?

Fill in the year. Then write the dates for October. Circle Columbus Day and Leif Ericson Day.

October 19 _____

Sun.	Mon.	Tues.	Wed.	Thurs.	Fri.	Sat.

True or False?

Take turns reading these sentences with a partner. Is each sentence true or false? Decide with your partner. Put an X under TRUE or FALSE.

		TRUE	FALSE
1.	Christopher Columbus was born in Spain.	_____	__X__
2.	The king and queen of Spain helped Columbus.	_____	_____
3.	Columbus wanted to bring gold and spices from Asia to Europe.	_____	_____
4.	Columbus died a rich and famous man.	_____	_____
5.	Only people in New York City celebrate Columbus Day.	_____	_____
6.	Columbus Day is a legal holiday in many states.	_____	_____
7.	Leif Ericson helped Columbus find the Bahamas.	_____	_____

Understanding Time Order

Take turns reading these sentences with a partner. Decide together what happened first, second, third, and so on. Put the sentences in order from 1 to 8.

_____ The first Columbus Day celebration was in New York City.

_____ President Lyndon Johnson made October 9 Leif Ericson Day.

_____ Columbus asked the king and queen of Spain for money for his trip.

_____ Columbus came to the New World.

_____ Columbus sailed from Spain to find Asia.

_____ Columbus learned to sail.

___1___ Leif Ericson came to the New World.

_____ Columbus was born in Italy.

BEFORE YOU CONTINUE

- Look at your guesses on page 99. Were you right?
- Now fill in Columbus Day on the Holiday Chart on page 154.

TALK ABOUT IT

Talk to a partner about a place he or she visited. Ask these questions and write the answers on the line. Then share the answers with the class.

Partner's Name: _____

1. Where did you go? _____

   _____

2. When did you go? _____

   _____

3. How did you get there? _____

   _____

4. How long did it take to get there? _____

   _____

5. How long did you stay? _____

   _____

6. What did you do? _____

_____

_____

7. What did you buy? _____

_____

_____

8. What did you like best? _____

_____

_____

9. What is another place you want to visit? _____

_____

_____

WRITE

A student from Vietnam wrote about a trip to Washington, D.C. Read her story.

Washington, D.C.

I went to Washington, D.C., with my family last June. We drove from Chicago, and it took 14 hours. What a long drive!

We stayed in Washington for 10 days. For three days, we went sightseeing. We saw the White House and the Capitol. We also went to Mount Vernon to see George Washington's house. We bought some souvenirs to bring home.

Then we visited relatives for a week. It was really good to see our relatives again. We had a wonderful trip. Maybe we'll go to Washington, D.C., again next summer!

Now write about a trip you took. Look at the questions on pages 104–105 and at the story above if you need help.

_____

_____

_____

_____

_____

_____

_____

BEFORE YOU READ

Talk about this photograph. Guess the answers to the questions below. Write your guesses on the lines.

1. Where is this child? _____

   _____

2. What is he wearing? _____

   _____

3. Why is he holding a bag? _____

   _____

Now turn the page and read.

Halloween

October 31 is Halloween. Halloween is not a national holiday, so people go to work. Children go to school. Halloween is a day to dress up and have fun. Children wear many different costumes. Some dress up as witches or ghosts. Other children wear animal costumes. Some dress up as TV characters. Parents make costumes for their children or buy costumes in stores.

Young children wear their costumes to school for class parties. After school, children go from house to house in their neighborhoods. Parents usually go with them. The children ring doorbells and say, "Trick or treat!" The treat is candy, fruit, or money. The child in the picture is trick-or-treating. He is carrying a bag for his treats.

Some adults like to dress up and go to Halloween parties too. But adults don't go from house to house and ask for candy!

Halloween means "holy evening." Halloween is the day before a religious day, All Saints' Day. On All Saints' Day, Christians remember dead family and friends. They go to church and to the cemetery.

Many years ago, people in Great Britain were afraid the night before All Saints' Day. They were afraid of bad spirits from dead people. They wanted to scare away the bad spirits, so they painted their faces. They wore their clothes inside out. They cut scary faces in pumpkins and put candles inside. Immigrants from Great Britain brought these Halloween customs to the United States.

Today people are not afraid on Halloween. Halloween is just for fun. People decorate their homes with witches, ghosts, and skeletons. They put scary pumpkins outside their houses. When Halloween is over, children are sad. They look forward to next year and a new costume. Only 364 days until next Halloween!

UNDERSTANDING NEW WORDS

Take turns reading these pairs of sentences with a partner. Is the meaning of the sentences the same or different? Decide with your partner. Circle SAME or DIFFERENT.

1. Halloween is a day to **dress up** and have fun.

   Halloween is a day to wear costumes.   (SAME)   DIFFERENT

2. Some children dress up as TV **characters.**

   Some children dress up as people or animals from TV.   SAME   DIFFERENT

3. Children ring doorbells and say, **"Trick or treat!"**

   Children ring doorbells and say, "Give me dinner!"   SAME   DIFFERENT

4. Many years ago on Halloween, people wanted to **scare away** the bad spirits.

   Many years ago on Halloween, people wanted to talk to the bad spirits.   SAME   DIFFERENT

5. Long ago in Great Britain, people wore their clothes **inside out** on Halloween.

   Long ago in Great Britain, people wore their clothes with the wrong side showing on Halloween.   SAME   DIFFERENT

6. People cut **scary** faces in pumpkins and put candles inside.

   People cut happy faces in pumpkins and put candles inside.   SAME   DIFFERENT

7. Children **look forward to** next Halloween and a new costume.

   Children wait happily for next Halloween and a new costume.   SAME   DIFFERENT

UNDERSTANDING WHAT YOU READ

When Is the Holiday?

Fill in the year. Then write the dates for October. Circle Halloween.

October 19 __

Sun.	Mon.	Tues.	Wed.	Thurs.	Fri.	Sat.

True or False?

Take turns reading these sentences with a partner. Is each sentence true or false? Decide with your partner. Put an X under TRUE or FALSE.

		TRUE	FALSE
1.	October 13 is Halloween.	_____	____X____
2.	Children wear costumes on Halloween.	_____	_____
3.	Parents buy or make costumes for their children.	_____	_____
4.	Some adults wear costumes on Halloween.	_____	_____
5.	Halloween is the day after All Saints' Day.	_____	_____
6.	People go to church on Halloween.	_____	_____
7.	Many years ago, people in Great Britain were afraid of bad spirits.	_____	_____

Understanding Sentences with Because

Take turns reading these sentences with a partner. Decide together how to finish each sentence. Cross out the letter of the answer. Then write the letter on the line.

1. Americans celebrate Halloween

   __c__

2. Young children wear costumes

   to school _____

3. Children say, "Trick or treat!"

   _____

4. *Halloween* means "holy

   evening" _____

5. Many years ago, people painted

   their faces _____

   a. because they want candy.

   b. because it is the night before All Saints' Day.

   ~~c~~ because immigrants from Great Britain brought Halloween customs to the U.S.

   d. because they wanted to scare away bad spirits.

   e. because they have class parties.

BEFORE YOU CONTINUE

- Look at your guesses on page 107. Were you right?
- Now fill in Halloween on the Holiday Chart on page 154.

TALK ABOUT IT

Most people are afraid of some things. Interview a partner about these ten things. Circle 1, 2, or 3.

Ask: "Are you afraid of *the dark?*"

Answer: "Yes, I'm *very afraid of* the dark."
         "I'm *just a little afraid of* the dark."
         "No, I'm *not at all afraid of* the dark."

Partner's Name: _____

	1 very afraid of	2 just a little afraid of	3 not at all afraid of
the dark	1	2	3
spiders	1	2	3
snakes	1	2	3
dogs	1	2	3
heights	1	2	3
swimming	1	2	3
flying	1	2	3
crowds	1	2	3
small places	1	2	3
elevators	1	2	3
(something else)	1	2	3
(something else)	1	2	3

Which three things on the chart is your partner most afraid of? Write them on the lines. Then share the answers with the class.

1. _____

2. _____

3. _____

 WRITE

Read the story and write in the missing words. Look at the words in the box below the story if you need help.

October 31 is ___Halloween___ . People decorate their houses
1

with pumpkins, witches, and _____ . Children and adults
2

like to wear _____ . They dress up and go to
3

_____ . Children go from house to house and ring
4

doorbells. They say, " _____ or treat!" Halloween is
5

_____ for everyone, young and old.
6

skeletons	parties	fun
Halloween	Trick	costumes

LET'S SING

On Halloween, many people decorate their stores and houses with pictures of skeletons. This is an old American folk song about skeleton bones.

Skeleton Bones

With the toe bone connected to the foot bone,
And the foot bone connected to the ankle bone,
And the ankle bone connected to the leg bone,
Oh goodness, they scare!

Oh those bones, oh those bones, oh those skeleton bones,
Oh those bones, oh those bones, oh those skeleton bones,
Oh those bones, oh those bones, oh those skeleton bones,
Oh goodness, they scare!

With the finger bone connected to the hand bone,
And the hand bone connected to the elbow bone,
And the elbow bone connected to the shoulder bone,
Oh goodness, they scare!

Oh those bones, oh those bones, oh those skeleton bones,
Oh those bones, oh those bones, oh those skeleton bones,
Oh those bones, oh those bones, oh those skeleton bones,
Oh goodness, they scare!

With the hip bone connected to the back bone,
And the back bone connected to the neck bone,
And the neck bone connected to the head bone,
Oh goodness, they scare!

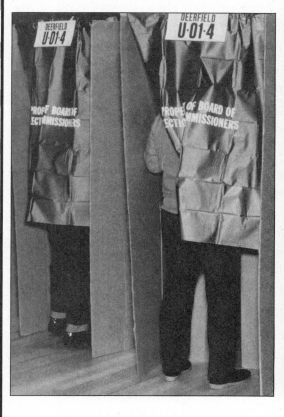
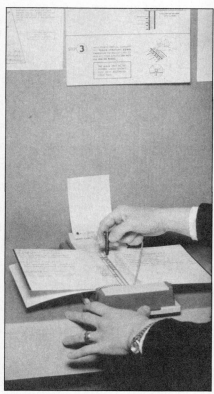

BEFORE YOU READ

Talk about these photographs. Guess the answers to the
questions below. Write your guesses on the lines.

1. Where are these people? _____

    _____

2. What are they doing? _____

    _____

3. What day is this? _____

    _____

*Now turn the
page and read.*

Election Day

Election Day is the Tuesday after the first Monday in November. For most people, Election Day is not a holiday from work or school. United States citizens vote on this day. Every four years, they vote for the President and Vice President of the United States. Every six years, they elect senators. Every two years, they elect representatives. On Election Day, many people also vote for city and state leaders.

The people in the picture are at a polling place. Polls are usually in schools, churches, and public buildings. On Election Day, polls are open from very early in the morning until 6:00 or 7:00 in the evening. People go to polling places near their homes. In the picture on the left, some people are voting in private voting booths. Most people use machines to vote. In the picture on the right, the person is using a voting machine. People always vote by secret ballot.

Today all United States citizens 18 and older can vote if they want to. But years ago, it was different. Women and African Americans did not have the right to vote. In 1871, black men received the right to vote. But many African Americans could not vote because of state laws about voting. For example, if people could not read or write, they could not vote in some states. These laws were very unfair.

In 1920, American women received the right to vote. In 1964, Congress passed the Civil Rights Act of 1964. This law gave voting rights to all United States citizens.

Today race and sex do not prevent Americans from voting or from running for political office. African Americans are now political leaders. Many cities have black mayors. In 1990, the state of Virginia elected the first black governor.

Women, too, are now political leaders. Many cities have women mayors, and some states have women governors. In 1984, a woman ran for Vice President. She lost the election, but this was an important step for American women. Maybe one day in the future, the United States will have a woman President.

UNDERSTANDING NEW WORDS

Take turns reading these sentences with a partner. Does **a**, **b**, or **c** have the same meaning as the sentence? Decide with your partner. Circle **a**, **b**, or **c**.

1. People vote in **private** voting booths.
   a. Many people are in the same voting booth.
   b. Only one person is in the voting booth.
   c. The voting booths are in the parking lot.

2. People always vote by **secret ballot**.
   a. Everybody pays to vote.
   b. Everybody knows your vote.
   c. Nobody knows your vote.

3. About 30 years ago, if people could not read or write, they could not vote in some states. These laws were very **unfair**.
   a. These laws were good.
   b. These laws were wrong.
   c. These laws were fair.

4. In 1964, Congress **passed** the Civil Rights Act of 1964.
   a. Congress talked about the new law.
   b. Congress voted against the new law.
   c. Congress voted yes for a new law.

5. Today race and sex do not **prevent** Americans from voting.
   a. Only whites can vote.
   b. All citizens 18 and older can vote.
   c. Only men can vote.

6. Today race and sex do not prevent Americans from **running** for political office.
   a. Anyone can vote.
   b. Only men can win elections.
   c. Any citizen can try to win an election.

UNDERSTANDING WHAT YOU READ

When Is the Holiday?

Fill in the year. Then write the dates for November. Circle Election Day.

November 19 ____

Sun.	Mon.	Tues.	Wed.	Thurs.	Fri.	Sat.

Correct the Sentences

Take turns reading these sentences with a partner. One word in each sentence is wrong. Correct each sentence with your partner. Write the new sentence on the line below.

1. Election Day is the Tuesday after the last Monday in November.

   Election Day is the Tuesday after the first Monday in November.

2. Every two years, Americans elect senators.

   _____

3. Polls are usually in supermarkets, churches, and public buildings.

   _____

   _____

4. In the picture, some people are waiting to drive.

   _____

5. Today all American citizens 21 and older can vote.

   _____

6. Women and children did not have the right to vote for many years.

   _____

   _____

7. In 1871, black men received the right to work.

   _____

8. In 1964, American women received the right to vote.

   _____

9. In 1984, a woman ran for Vice President, and she won the election.

   _____

   _____

Understanding Sentences with **Because**

Take turns reading these sentences with a partner. Decide together how to finish each sentence. Cross out the letter of the answer. Then write the letter on the line.

1. Election Day is an important day for American citizens ___C___

   a. because they are not 18 years old.

2. Americans vote in private voting booths _____

   b. because of laws from 1871, 1920, and 1964.

3. Citizens of any race or sex can vote _____

   ~~c~~ because they vote on this day.

4. For a long time, African Americans could not vote in some states _____

   d. because of unfair voting laws.

5. Most high-school students cannot vote _____

   e. because they always vote by secret ballot.

6. People usually go to work on Election Day _____

   f. because it is not a national holiday.

BEFORE YOU CONTINUE

- Look at your guesses on page 115. Were you right?
- Now fill in Election Day on the Holiday Chart on page 154.

TALK ABOUT IT, *Activity 1*

On Election Day, Americans do not vote only for political leaders. They also vote on issues such as taxes and gun control.

Talk about the issues below in a small group. Would you vote yes or no on each of these issues? Put an X under **Yes** or **No**. Try to agree on the same answer. Then share your answers with the class.

ISSUES	Yes	No
change the voting age from 18 to 21		
change the driving age from 16 to 21		
give the death penalty to drug dealers		
put marijuana smokers in jail		
make it illegal to buy or sell alcohol		
make it illegal to own a handgun		
take driver's licenses away from drunk drivers		
raise taxes to fight pollution		
raise taxes to have more money for the military		
raise taxes to have more money for the space program		

TALK ABOUT IT, *Activity 2*

Both Ben Losa and Maria Jones want to be the mayor of their city. In a small group, talk about these two candidates. Who will you vote for? Try to agree on the same answer. Then share your answer with the class.

BEN LOSA

- 45 years old
- married, four children
- 20-year resident of city
- restaurant owner
- high-school diploma and two years of college
- soccer coach, 10 years
- school board, 10 years

MARIA JONES

- 35 years old
- single
- 10-year resident of city
- accountant
- college graduate
- president of local Women in Business organization
- author of *Women Can Be Successful in Business*

Personal Statement: "This city is my home. I love this city. I know the people and their kids. I know the good things about living here, and I also know about the problems. I can speak for the people."

Personal Statement: "I know business, and I know this city. We have some problems, and I know how to fix them. I will make this a city to be proud of."

We are going to vote for _____ because

_____.

WRITE

Read the story and write in the missing words. Look at the words in the box below the story if you need help.

For many years, all Americans did not have the right to

___*vote*___ . Women could not vote. Many _____
    1   2

Americans could not vote. Slowly, the voting laws changed. In 1920,

_____ received the right to vote. In 1964, Congress passed
    3

the Civil Rights Act of 1964 to give voting rights to all U.S. citizens.

Today all U.S. _____ 18 years and older can
                                         4

vote. Voting is always by _____ ballot. Race and
                                               5

_____ do not prevent people from voting or from running
    6

for political office.

citizens	sex	secret
African	vote	women

LET'S SING

People sing this song at election time. They usually sing this song to winners, but they sometimes sing it to losers too.

For He's a Jolly Good Fellow

For a man:

> For he's a jolly good fellow,
> For he's a jolly good fellow,
> For he's a jolly good fellow,
> Which nobody can deny.
> Which nobody can deny.
> Which nobody can deny.
> For he's a jolly good fellow,
> Which nobody can deny.

For a woman:

> For she's a jolly good person,
> For she's a jolly good person,
> For she's a jolly good person,
> Which nobody can deny.
> Which nobody can deny.
> Which nobody can deny.
> For she's a jolly good person,
> Which nobody can deny.

BEFORE YOU READ

Talk about this photograph. Guess the answers to the questions below. Write your guesses on the lines.

1. Who are these people? _____

   _____

2. Where are they? _____

   _____

3. What are they doing? _____

Now turn the page and read.

   _____

Veterans Day

November 11 is a national holiday. On this day, Americans remember all veterans, living and dead. Veterans are men and women from the armed forces such as the army and the navy. Many veterans served their country during wars. Others served during times of peace.

Veterans Day is not a day for parties. People do not eat special food or give gifts on this day. Instead, they watch Veterans Day parades and go to public ceremonies. Many people also go to cemeteries on this day. They put flowers on veterans' graves.

Americans bury many veterans in Arlington National Cemetery in Virginia. There are four special soldiers in this cemetery. One soldier fought in World War I. One fought in World War II. One fought in the Korean War. And one fought in the Vietnam War. Nobody knows their names, so people call their grave the Tomb of the Unknowns. The President or Vice President puts flowers at this tomb each Veterans Day to honor all veterans. The picture shows a Veterans Day ceremony at the Tomb of the Unknowns.

Americans remember the end of World War I on Veterans Day. World War I started in 1914. England, Russia, France, and the United States fought Germany, Austria-Hungary, and Italy. Thousands of soldiers died. The war ended on November 11, 1918, when Germany signed an armistice, or peace agreement. In 1919, President Woodrow Wilson named November 11 Armistice Day.

Armistice Day became a national holiday in 1938. In 1954, Congress changed the name to Veterans Day. Today Americans remember all veterans on Veterans Day.

Some people don't think about veterans on November 11. They think of the day as a holiday from work or school. They go to big sales at stores. But Veterans Day is a day for Americans to remember war and to hope for peace.

UNDERSTANDING NEW WORDS

Take turns reading these sentences and the words below with a partner. Decide together how to finish each sentence. Write the words on the line.

1. Veterans are men and women from _the armed forces._ .
    the armed forces
    the post office
    politics

2. Some people go to public _____ on November 11.
    parties
    ceremonies
    wars

3. Many people go to _____ on Veterans Day.
    cemeteries
    war
    the bank

4. People put flowers on veterans' _____ on Veterans Day.
    armed forces
    cars
    graves

5. Americans _____ many veterans in Arlington National Cemetery.
    bury
    wake up
    fight

6. The President or Vice President puts flowers at the _____ of the Unknowns.
    parades
    Tomb
    armistice

UNDERSTANDING WHAT YOU READ

When Is the Holiday?

Fill in the year. Then write the dates for November. Circle Veterans Day.

November 19 _____

Sun.	Mon.	Tues.	Wed.	Thurs.	Fri.	Sat.

Correct the Sentences

Take turns reading these sentences with a partner. One word in each sentence is wrong. Correct each sentence with your partner. Write the new sentence on the line below.

1. November 1 is a national holiday.

   November 11 is a national holiday.

2. Americans bury many politicians in Arlington National Cemetery.

   _____

3. There are four special soldiers in this cemetery, and everybody knows their names.

   _____

4. The President or Vice President puts guns at the Tomb of the Unknowns to honor all veterans.

   _____

5. World War II ended on November 11, 1918.

_____

6. President Woodrow Wilson named November 11 Veterans Day.

_____

Fact or Opinion?

Take turns reading these sentences with a partner. Is each sentence fact or opinion? Decide with your partner. Put an *X* under FACT or OPINION.

		FACT	OPINION
1.	Many veterans served their country during wars.	X	
2.	Male veterans are more important than female veterans.		
3.	Many people visit cemeteries on Veterans Day.		
4.	Veterans Day is more important than Christmas.		
5.	Some people go shopping on Veterans Day and don't think about veterans.		

BEFORE YOU CONTINUE

- Look at your guesses on page 125. Were you right?
- Now fill in Veterans Day on the Holiday Chart on page 155.

TALK ABOUT IT

Interview a partner about the armed forces in his or her native country. Write your partner's answers on the lines. Then share the answers with the class.

Partner's Name: _____

1. Does your native country have a special day to honor veterans? When is it? What is the name of the day?

   _____

   _____

2. Does everyone in your native country serve in the armed forces? Who serves? How old are they?

   _____

   _____

3. Do you think women should serve in the armed forces? Why or why not?

   _____

   _____

4. Do you think there will be another world war? Why or why not?

   _____

   _____

WRITE

Read the story and write in the missing words. Look at the words in the box below the story if you need help.

November 11 is Veterans Day in the United States. This
         1

day honors _____ and women from the _____
                 2   3

forces. The first name for Veterans Day was _____ Day.
                                                    4

Congress changed the name in _____ because there were
                                      5

more wars. Today Americans honor all _____ on Veterans
                                             6

Day.

armed	November	men
1954	Armistice	veterans

A famous American folksinger, Pete Seeger, wrote this song. He got the idea from an old Ukrainian folk song.

Where Have All the Flowers Gone?

Where have all the flowers gone,
Long time passing?
Where have all the flowers gone,
Long time ago?
Where have all the flowers gone?
Young girls picked them every one.
When will they ever learn?
When will they ever learn?

Where have all the young girls gone,
Long time passing?
Where have all the young girls gone,
Long time ago?
Where have all the young girls gone?
Gone to young men every one.
When will they ever learn?
When will they ever learn?

Where have all the young men gone,
Long time passing?
Where have all the young men gone,
Long time ago?
Where have all the young men gone?
They are all in uniform.
When will they ever learn?
When will they ever learn?

Where have all the soldiers gone,
Long time passing?
Where have all the soldiers gone,
Long time ago?
Where have all the soldiers gone?
Gone to graveyards every one.
When will they ever learn?
When will they ever learn?

Where have all the graveyards gone,
Long time passing?
Where have all the graveyards gone,
Long time ago?
Where have all the graveyards gone?
Covered with flowers every one.
When will they ever learn?
When will they ever learn?

Where have all the flowers gone,
Ooooo . . .
Where have all the flowers gone,
Long time ago?
Where have all the flowers gone?
Young girls picked them every one.
When will they ever learn?
When will they ever learn?

17

BEFORE YOU READ

Talk about this photograph. Guess the answers to the questions below. Write your guesses on the lines.

1. Who are these people? _____

   _____

2. What are they going to eat? _____

   _____

3. Why are they together? _____

   _____

133

Thanksgiving Day

The fourth Thursday in November is Thanksgiving. Thanksgiving is a national holiday, so most people don't go to work. People get together with their families and friends to give thanks for the good things in their lives. Many people travel by plane, train, bus, or car to be with their relatives. More people travel for Thanksgiving than for any other holiday.

On Thanksgiving Day, families come together for a special dinner. The family in the picture is together for Thanksgiving dinner. They are going to eat turkey, stuffing, mashed potatoes, and cranberries. They will have pumpkin pie for dessert. After dinner, the family will relax and talk. Some of them will watch a football game on TV.

Thanksgiving started over 350 years ago with the Pilgrims. In the fall of 1620, one hundred Pilgrims came to the United States from England. They came on a boat, the *Mayflower*. Half of the people came for religious freedom. All came for new lives.

The first winter, the Pilgrims were hungry, sick, and cold. Many people died. Then the Native Americans, the Indians, helped the Pilgrims. They taught the Pilgrims to plant corn and build houses. In the fall of 1621, the Pilgrims and the Indians had the first Thanksgiving. The Pilgrims wanted to give thanks for their new land. They also wanted to thank the Indians for their help.

The first Thanksgiving was three days long. The picture on the next page shows the Native Americans and the Pilgrims celebrating together. But in the years after the first Thanksgiving, there were many problems between the newcomers and the Indians. The newcomers took land from the Indians. They killed Indians and destroyed the Native American way of life. Today many Americans feel ashamed about this. Some states celebrate Native American days. On these days, Americans honor Native Americans and remember the peace and friendship of the first Thanksgiving.

UNDERSTANDING NEW WORDS

Take turns reading these sentences with a partner. Does **a, b,** or **c** mean the same as the underlined word? Decide with your partner. Circle **a, b,** or **c.**

1. Many people travel by plane, train, bus, or car to be with their <u>relatives</u> on Thanksgiving.
   - **a.** neighbors
   - **b.** families
   - **c.** employers

2. After Thanksgiving dinner, people <u>relax</u> and talk.
   - **a.** rest
   - **b.** work
   - **c.** clean

3. Newcomers killed American Indians and <u>destroyed</u> the Native American way of life.
   - **a.** helped
   - **b.** ruined
   - **c.** built

4. In the years after the first Thanksgiving, newcomers took land from the Native Americans and killed them. Today many Americans feel <u>ashamed</u> about this.
   - **a.** happy
   - **b.** good
   - **c.** sorry

UNDERSTANDING WHAT YOU READ

When Is the Holiday?

Fill in the year. Then write the dates for November. Circle Thanksgiving.

November 19_____

Sun.	Mon.	Tues.	Wed.	Thurs.	Fri.	Sat.

True or False?

Take turns reading these sentences with a partner. Is each sentence true or false? Decide with your partner. Put an X under TRUE or FALSE.

		TRUE	FALSE
1.	The fourth Tuesday in November is Thanksgiving.	_____	__X__
2.	More people travel for Thanksgiving than for any other holiday.	_____	_____
3.	On Thanksgiving, families come together for a special dinner.	_____	_____
4.	Thanksgiving started over 350 years ago with the Pilgrims.	_____	_____

5. In the fall of 1600, a thousand   _____   _____
    Pilgrims came to the United States
    from England.

6. All of the Pilgrims came for   _____   _____
    religious freedom.

7. The first Thanksgiving was in the   _____   _____
    fall of 1621.

8. On the first Thanksgiving, the   _____   _____
    Indians thanked the Pilgrims for
    their help.

9. Newcomers to the United States   _____   _____
    were always friendly and kind to
    the Native Americans.

10. Americans today celebrate Native   _____   _____
    American days to honor the
    Pilgrims.

Understanding Time Order

Take turns reading these sentences with a partner. Decide together what happened first, second, third, and so on. Put the sentences in order from 1 to 7.

_____ People travel by plane, train, car, or bus for Thanksgiving dinner with relatives.

_____ The Pilgrims came to the United States on the *Mayflower*.

_____ The American Indians helped the Pilgrims grow food and build houses.

_____ Newcomers took land from the Native Americans and killed them.

___**1**__ The Pilgrims were unhappy in England.

_____ Many Pilgrims died during the first winter because they were sick and hungry.

_____ The Pilgrims and the Indians celebrated the first Thanksgiving.

BEFORE YOU CONTINUE

- Look at your guesses on page 133. Were you right?
- Now fill in Thanksgiving Day on the Holiday Chart on page 155.

TALK ABOUT IT, *Activity 1*

Pilgrim farmers had to eat a lot of food to be strong. They ate 6,000 calories a day. Now 2,000 calories a day are enough for most people.

Many Americans worry about eating too much. They watch their weight and go on diets.

You and your partner are on diets. You want to know how many calories Thanksgiving dinner has. Ask your partner questions to finish the chart. *Do not* look at your partner's book.

Example: "What has <u>240</u> calories?"
            "How many calories does <u>turkey</u> have?"

Food (for one person)	Calories
turkey	240
stuffing	300
cranberry sauce	
mashed potatoes	150
green beans	50
roll and butter	
	150
pumpkin pie with whipped cream	440

How many calories are in Thanksgiving dinner? _____

TALK ABOUT IT, *Activity 1*

Pilgrim farmers had to eat a lot of food to be strong. They ate 6,000 calories a day. Now 2,000 calories a day are enough for most people.

Many Americans worry about eating too much. They watch their weight and go on diets.

You and your partner are on diets. You want to know how many calories Thanksgiving dinner has. Ask your partner questions to finish the chart. *Do not* look at your partner's book.

Example: "What has 240 calories?"
"How many calories does turkey have?"

Food (for one person)	Calories
turkey	240
stuffing	
cranberry sauce	100
mashed potatoes	
	50
roll and butter	180
glass of wine	150
	440

How many calories are in Thanksgiving dinner? _____

TALK ABOUT IT, *Activity 2*

People are very busy on Thanksgiving Day. On the top of the next page are some things they do. Talk with a partner or a small group about these things to do. Decide together what to do first, second, third, and so on. Put these things to do in order from 1 to 8.

_____ In the morning, put the turkey in the oven.

_____ Call the family to the table.

_____ Eat the turkey.

_____ Sit down to eat.

_____ Eat pumpkin pie.

__1__ Get up early.

_____ Take the turkey out of the oven.

_____ Wash all the dishes.

WRITE

A student from Laos is thankful for many things. Read her story.

I am thankful for my family. My husband and I have good jobs in our new country. We are healthy. We have a nice apartment. It is clean and warm. The neighbors are friendly.

What are you thankful for? Write four things. Use the words in the box below if you need help. Then share your answers with the class.

1. _____

2. _____

3. _____

4. _____

friends	family	job
school	parents	food
health	children	home
church	money	freedom

LET'S SING

Today most Americans travel by car, plane, train, or bus to be with their families on Thanksgiving. But many years ago, people traveled by horse. In the winter, horses pulled sleighs in the snow.

This is an old American folk song about Thanksgiving. A family is going to visit their grandmother for Thanksgiving dinner. They are riding in a sleigh.

Over the River and Through the Woods

Over the river and through the woods
To grandmother's house we go.
The horse knows the way to carry the sleigh
Through the white and drifted snow.
Over the river and through the woods
Oh how the wind does blow!
It stings the toes and bites the nose
As over the ground we go.

Over the river and through the woods
Trot fast my dapple gray!
Spring over the ground like a hunting hound
For this is Thanksgiving Day!
Over the river and through the woods,
Now grandfather's face I spy!
Hurrah for the fun! Is the turkey done?
Hurrah for the pumpkin pie!

BEFORE YOU READ

Talk about this photograph. Guess the answers to the questions below. Write your guesses on the lines.

1. Who are these people? _____

   _____

2. Where are they? _____

   _____

3. What is the little girl saying to the man? _____

   _____

Now turn the page and read.

Christmas

December 25 is Christmas. Christmas is both a national holiday and a religious holiday. Christians remember the birth of Jesus Christ on Christmas. Many non-Christians celebrate Christmas too.

The Christmas season starts after Thanksgiving, in late November. Christmas is a time for giving presents to friends, family, and poor people. Churches, businesses, and other groups give money, food, and toys to needy families.

Some people make gifts, but most people buy presents in stores. Stores get very crowded around Christmas. There are shoppers everywhere! Stores have beautiful decorations in Christmas colors of red and green.

Many people decorate their homes at Christmas. They buy trees and decorate them with electric lights and ornaments. Some people put electric lights outside their houses. At Christmas, neighborhoods are beautiful with many bright Christmas lights.

Jewish people have a Festival of Lights in December. For eight days, Jewish people light candles and give gifts. This festival, Hanukkah, is a joyful holiday.

Before Christmas or Hanukkah, people send greeting cards to friends and relatives. These cards say "Season's Greetings," "Happy Holidays" or "Merry Christmas." People also bake cookies to share with friends and neighbors.

Christmas Eve is the night before Christmas. Children believe a fat, jolly man brings gifts on Christmas Eve. His name is Santa Claus. During the weeks before Christmas, parents bring their children to see Santa. Many stores have a Santa Claus for children to visit. The little girl in the picture is telling Santa about a teddy. She wants a teddy for Christmas. Santa tells her, "Ho, ho, ho, and a Merry Christmas!"

Late on Christmas Eve, Santa comes down the chimney and puts presents under the tree. He also puts gifts in children's stockings. On Christmas morning, children look under the tree and in their stockings for gifts from Santa Claus.

Many people go to church on Christmas Eve or Christmas Day. They sing joyful songs, Christmas carols. On Christmas Day, families open gifts and eat a holiday dinner together.

UNDERSTANDING NEW WORDS

Take turns reading these sentences and the words below with a partner.
Decide together how to finish each sentence. Write the word on the line.

1. The Christmas ___*season*___ starts after Thanksgiving, in late
    November.
    week
    season
    month

2. Churches, businesses, and other groups give money, food, and

    toys to _____ families.
    rich
    angry
    needy

3. Stores get very _____ around Christmas.
    crowded
    quiet
    expensive

4. People buy trees and decorate them with electric lights and

    _____ .
    presents
    ornaments
    cookies

5. Before Christmas, people send _____ to
    friends and relatives.
    Santa Claus
    Christmas lights
    greeting cards

6. Children believe a fat, _____ man brings gifts on
    Christmas Eve.
    jolly
    angry
    sad

7. On Christmas Day, Christians go to church and sing joyful songs.

   These songs are Christmas _____ .
       carols
       stockings
       presents

8. Hanukkah and Christmas are _____ holidays.
       Christian
       joyful
       sad

UNDERSTANDING WHAT YOU READ

When Is the Holiday?

Fill in the year. Then write the dates for December. Circle Christmas Eve and Christmas Day.

December 19 ____

Sun.	Mon.	Tues.	Wed.	Thurs.	Fri.	Sat.

Correct the Sentences

Take turns reading these sentences with a partner. One word in each sentence is wrong. Correct each sentence together. Write the new sentence on the line below.

1. Christians remember the death of Jesus Christ on Christmas.

   Christians remember the birth of Jesus Christ on Christmas.

2. The Christmas season starts after Thanksgiving, in late October.

   _____

3. Christmas is a time for giving presents to friends, family, and rich people.

_____

_____

4. Stores have beautiful decorations in Christmas colors of red and blue.

_____

_____

5. Jewish people celebrate Hanukkah for four days.

_____

6. Greeting cards say, "Happy Christmas," or "Merry Christmas."

_____

7. During the weeks before Christmas, parents bring their children to see doctors.

_____

_____

8. Children believe a fat, jolly man sells gifts on Christmas Eve.

_____

9. Santa puts presents under the Christmas tree and in children's coats.

_____

_____

10. Many Christians go to school on Christmas Eve or Christmas Day.

_____

BEFORE YOU CONTINUE

- Look at your guesses on page 143. Were you right?
- Now fill in Christmas on the Holiday Chart on page 155.

TALK ABOUT IT, *Activity 1*

Talk about these things with a partner or a small group. Six things are not related to Christmas. One is crossed out. Cross out five more. Then share your answers with the class.

~~flags~~	presents
joyful	Santa Claus
carols	cookies
cemeteries	ornaments
yellow	red and green
pizza	picnics
stockings	trees
colored eggs	electric lights

TALK ABOUT IT, *Activity 2*

You and a friend want to get together for dinner during the Christmas season. Look at your calendar for December. Ask your partner questions to find a date you can meet. *Do not* look at your partner's book.

Ask: "Are you free on <u>Tuesday, December 3</u>?"
       "How about <u>Tuesday, December 3</u>?"

Answer: "I can't make it then. <u>I have ESL class.</u>"
          "That's not a good day. <u>I have ESL class.</u>"

DECEMBER

SUNDAY	MONDAY	TUESDAY	WEDNESDAY	THURSDAY	FRIDAY	SATURDAY
1	2 ESL CLASS	3	4 ESL CLASS	5	6 CHRISTMAS PARTY	7
8	9 ESL CLASS	10	11 ESL CLASS	12	13	14
15	16 CHRISTMAS SHOPPING	17 CHRISTMAS SHOPPING	18	19 DECORATE CHRISTMAS TREE	20	21 BAKE COOKIES
22	23 GROCERY SHOPPING	24 CHURCH AT 5:00	25	26	27 VACATION →	28
29	30 VACATION	31 ← →				

DATE FOR DINNER: _____

TALK ABOUT IT, *Activity 2*

You and a friend want to get together for dinner during the Christmas season. Look at your calendar for December. Ask your partner questions to find a date you can meet. *Do not* look at your partner's book.

Ask: "Are you free on <u>Monday, December 2</u>?"
      "How about <u>Monday, December 2</u>?"

Answer: "I can't make it then. <u>I have ESL class</u>."
        "That's not a good day. <u>I have ESL class</u>."

DECEMBER

SUNDAY	MONDAY	TUESDAY	WEDNESDAY	THURSDAY	FRIDAY	SATURDAY
1 CHRISTMAS SHOPPING	2	3 ESL CLASS	4	5 ESL CLASS	6	7 BAKE COOKIES
8 BUY CHRISTMAS TREE	9	10 ESL CLASS	11	12 ESL CLASS	13 SHOP WITH MOM	14 CHRISTMAS PARTY
15 SEE SANTA CLAUS	16	17	18 DECORATE HOUSE	19	20	21
22 WRAP PRESENTS	23	24	25 DINNER AT GRANDMA'S	26	27	28
29	30	31				

DATE FOR DINNER: _____

WRITE

Americans often send holiday newsletters with their cards. These letters tell the news of the past year. People write about their families, jobs, and vacations.

Read Marta's holiday newsletter to her aunt in New York.

December 15, 1991

Dear Aunt Connie,

Merry Christmas to you and your family! This past year was very busy. In September, I started a new teaching job. The boys are playing soccer after school. Last April, Miguel went to France for his job. He loved it!

We took a family vacation to Disneyland last summer. Everyone had fun. Maybe next summer we will come and visit you in New York!

We hope you and your family are well. Don't forget, you are always welcome to visit us in California.

Love,
Marta

Now write a letter about last year. Then share your letter with the class.

_____

_____

_____

_____

_____

_____

_____

During the Christmas season, you hear Christmas carols everywhere—in stores, in banks, and on the streets. Here are two famous Christmas carols.

Jingle Bells

Dashing through the snow
In a one-horse open sleigh,
O'er the fields we go
Laughing all the way.

Bells on bobtail ring
Making spirits bright,
What fun it is to ride and sing
A sleighing song tonight!

Jingle bells, jingle bells,
Jingle all the way!
Oh what fun it is to ride
In a one-horse open sleigh!

Jingle bells, jingle bells,
Jingle all the way!
Oh what fun it is to ride
In a one-horse open sleigh!

Silent Night

Silent night, holy night
All is calm, all is bright.
Round yon virgin, mother and child,
Holy infant so tender and mild,
Sleep in heavenly peace,
Sleep in heavenly peace.

Silent night, holy night
Shepherds quake at the sight.
Glory streams from heaven afar.
Heavenly hosts sing Hallelujah.
Christ the Savior is born!
Christ the Savior is born!

Holiday Chart

Holiday	When Is the Holiday?	What Do Americans Do?	What Do Americans Say?
New Year's Eve			
New Year's Day			
Martin Luther King, Jr., Day			
Valentine's Day			
Presidents' Day			
St. Patrick's Day			
April Fools' Day			
Easter			

Holiday	When Is the Holiday?	What Do Americans Do?	What Do Americans Say?
Mother's Day			
Father's Day			
Memorial Day			
Flag Day			
Independence Day (Fourth of July)			
Labor Day			
Columbus Day			
Halloween			
Election Day			

Holiday	When Is the Holiday?	What Do Americans Do?	What Do Americans Say?
Veterans Day			
Thanksgiving Day			
Christmas			

Holiday Expressions

U.S. Holiday	Expression
New Year's Eve and New Year's Day	Happy New Year
Martin Luther King, Jr., Day	No Expression
Valentine's Day	Happy Valentine's Day
Presidents' Day	No Expression
St. Patrick's Day	Happy St. Patrick's Day
April Fools' Day	April Fool
Easter	Happy Easter
Mother's Day	Happy Mother's Day
Father's Day	Happy Father's Day
Memorial Day	No Expression
Flag Day	No Expression
Independence Day (Fourth of July)	No Expression
Labor Day	No Expression
Columbus Day	No Expression
Halloween	Happy Halloween Trick or Treat
Election Day	No Expression
Veterans Day	No Expression
Thanksgiving Day	Happy Thanksgiving
Christmas	Merry Christmas Happy Holidays

Answer Key

CHAPTER 1 NEW YEAR'S EVE AND NEW YEAR'S DAY

Understanding New Words (page 3)

2. Same   3. Different   4. Same   5. Same

New Year's Eve or New Year's Day? (page 5)

2. New Year's Day   3. New Year's Eve   4. New Year's Eve
5. New Year's Day   6. New Year's Day   7. New Year's Eve
8. New Year's Eve

True or False? (page 6)

2. False   3. True   4. False   5. True

Understanding Sentences with Because (page 6)

2. e   3. d   4. b   5. a

CHAPTER 2 MARTIN LUTHER KING, JR., DAY

Understanding New Words (page 11)

2. Same   3. Different   4. Same

True or False? (page 12)

2. False   3. False   4. True   5. False
6. False   7. False   8. True

Write (page 15)

2. restaurants   3. vote   4. Martin Luther King, Jr.
5. Peace   6. rights

CHAPTER 3 VALENTINE'S DAY

Understanding New Words (page 19)

2. a   3. b   4. a

Correct the Sentences (page 20)

2. Children and friends usually give each other <u>humorous</u> cards on Valentine's Day.
3. Children give <u>cards</u> to their friends at school parties.
4. Many people <u>give red</u> roses to people they love.
5. On February 15 in Roman times, young <u>men</u> chose their sweethearts for the year.
6. Americans spend <u>millions</u> of dollars on valentine cards and gifts each year.

True or False? (page 21)

2. False   3. True   4. False   5. False

CHAPTER 4 PRESIDENTS' DAY

Understanding New Words (page 27)

2. c   3. a   4. c
5. b   6. a

Washington or Lincoln? (page 29)

2. Lincoln   3. Lincoln   4. Lincoln
5. Washington   6. Lincoln   7. Washington
8. Lincoln   9. Washington   10. Washington

Understanding Time Order (page 30)

2. Washington became the first President.
3. Washington died at Mount Vernon.
4. Lincoln was born in Kentucky.
5. Lincoln became a lawyer.
6. Lincoln freed many slaves.
7. A man assassinated Lincoln in Washington, D.C.
8. Presidents' Day became a national holiday.

CHAPTER 5 ST. PATRICK'S DAY

Understanding New Words (page 37)

2. a   3. a   4. b

Correct the Sentences (pages 38–39)

2. On St. Patrick's Day, many people eat <u>Irish</u> food.
3. There are no <u>snakes</u> in Ireland because St. Patrick sent them away.
4. St. Patrick's Day celebrations helped the Irish <u>remember</u> their country, their music, and their families.
5. Chinese people celebrate Chinese New Year in January or <u>February</u>.
6. On *Cinco de mayo*, many people eat <u>Mexican</u> food.
7. Today's <u>immigrants</u> to the United States bring celebrations with them.

Understanding Sentences with Because (page 39)

2. c   3. b   4. f
5. a   6. e

Write (page 41)

2. green   3. parades   4. Immigrants
5. celebrate   6. parties

CHAPTER 6 APRIL FOOLS' DAY

Understanding New Words (page 45)

2. b   3. b   4. a   5. b

Understanding Questions with When (page 46)

2. April Fools' Day is April 1.
3. Nobody knows when April Fools' Day started.
4. Some people think April Fools' Day started in the 1500s in France.
5. People in Mexico celebrate Fools' Day on December 28.

CHAPTER 7 EASTER

Understanding New Words (page 51)

2. b   3. b   4. a   5. a

Correct the Sentences (page 53)

2. The word *Easter* comes from the name of a goddess of spring and <u>light</u>.
3. Many people <u>wear</u> new clothes on Easter Sunday.
4. The night before Easter, the Easter <u>bunny</u> visits many homes.
5. On Easter morning, <u>children</u> look for eggs from the Easter bunny.
6. Many schools and <u>businesses</u> close on Good Friday.
7. Easter is a very <u>joyful</u> holiday for Christians.
8. For <u>eight</u> days, Jewish people celebrate Passover.

Talk About It, Activity 1 (page 54)

2. flags
3. Christmas carols
4. picnics
5. hamburgers
6. electric lights

Talk About It, Activity 2 (page 55)

2. Buy eggs and a coloring kit.
3. Read the directions on the kit.
4. Hard-boil the eggs.
5. Cool the eggs.
6. Mix water, vinegar, and dye in small cups.
7. Put the eggs in the small cups with the dye.
8. Let the eggs dry.
9. Put the eggs in a basket.

CHAPTER 8 MOTHER'S DAY AND FATHER'S DAY

Understanding New Words (page 59)

2. a
3. a
4. b
5. b

Correct the Sentences (page 61)

2. People give cards and flowers to their mothers and grandmothers on <u>Mother's</u> Day.
3. Many families go to a <u>restaurant</u> for brunch or dinner on Mother's Day.
4. Anna Jarvis, a <u>woman</u> from West Virginia, first thought of Mother's Day.
5. Father's Day is the third <u>Sunday</u> in June.
6. When Sonora Dodd was a young girl, her <u>mother</u> died.
7. Sonora Dodd wanted to honor her father for his <u>hard</u> work and love.
8. The first Father's Day was in 1910 in Washington <u>State</u>.

CHAPTER 9 MEMORIAL DAY

Understanding New Words (page 67)

2. a   3. a   4. b
5. a   6. b

Correct the Sentences (pages 68–69)

2. In the picture, a child is putting <u>flowers</u> on his grandfather's grave.
3. The first Memorial Day was many years ago, after the <u>Civil</u> War.
4. After the Civil War, people wanted to remember the <u>dead</u>.
5. In 1866, people began to decorate the <u>graves</u> of Civil War soldiers.
6. American veterans from World War I began to sell <u>poppies</u> on Decoration Day.
7. Veterans today sell poppies for Memorial Day, and the money helps poor and sick <u>veterans</u>.
8. Memorial Day is a <u>three</u>-day weekend for most Americans.
9. On Memorial Day, people go on picnics and enjoy the <u>warm</u> weather.

Understanding Sentences with So (page 70)

2. d   3. a   4. b   5. e

Talk About It, Activity 1 (page 71)

2. candy   3. presents   4. popcorn
5. radio   6. turkey

CHAPTER 10 FLAG DAY

Understanding New Words (page 77)

2. a   3. a   4. b
5. a   6. a   7. a

Understanding Sentences with Because (page 78)

2. b   3. d   4. e   5. a

Understanding Time Order (page 79)

2. The flag had 15 stars and 15 stripes.
3. Francis Scott Key wrote "The Star-Spangled Banner."
4. A store in Detroit made a huge flag.
5. Alaska joined the United States.
6. The flag has 50 stars.

Write (page 81)

2. original   3. joined   4. star
5. anthem   6. sing

CHAPTER 11 INDEPENDENCE DAY

Understanding New Words (page 85)

2. c   3. c   4. c   5. b

True or False? (pages 86–87)

2. True   3. False   4. False
5. True   6. True   7. False
8. True   9. True   10. False

Understanding Sentences with So (page 87)

2. c   3. a   4. e   5. d

Talk About It, Activity 2 (page 89)

2. jail   3. turkey   4. church
5. snow   6. Canada

Write (page 89)

2. England   3. outside   4. parades
5. fireworks   6. freedom

CHAPTER 12 LABOR DAY

Understanding New Words (page 93)

2. b   3. b   4. a   5. a

Correct the Sentences (page 94)

2. Many people <u>worked</u> seven days a week, but they made very little money.
3. Workers didn't want to <u>lose</u> their jobs.
4. Through the unions, workers <u>slowly</u> changed their lives.
5. Sometimes <u>workers</u> went on strike for better pay.
6. Peter J. McGuire was the president of a <u>union</u>.
7. Labor Day is always the <u>first</u> Monday in September.

Understanding Sentences with **Because** (page 95)

2. d   3. e   4. a   5. c

CHAPTER 13 COLUMBUS DAY

Understanding New Words (page 101)
2. Different   3. Same   4. Same

True or False? (page 102)
2. True   3. True   4. False
5. False   6. True   7. False

Understanding Time Order (page 103)
2. Columbus was born in Italy.
3. Columbus learned to sail.
4. Columbus asked the king and queen of Spain for money for his trip.
5. Columbus sailed from Spain to find Asia.
6. Columbus came to the New World.
7. The first Columbus Day celebration was in New York City.
8. President Lyndon Johnson made October 9 Leif Ericson Day.

CHAPTER 14 HALLOWEEN

Understanding New Words (page 109)
2. Same   3. Different   4. Different
5. Same   6. Different   7. Same

True or False? (page 110)
2. True   3. True   4. True
5. False   6. False   7. True

Understanding Sentences with Because (page 111)
2. e   3. a   4. b   5. d

Write (page 113)
2. skeletons   3. costumes   4. parties
5. Trick   6. fun

CHAPTER 15 ELECTION DAY

Understanding New Words (page 117)
2. c   3. b   4. c
5. b   6. c

Correct the Sentences (pages 118–119)

2. Every two years, Americans elect <u>representatives</u>.
    or
    Every <u>six</u> years, Americans elect senators.

3. Polls are usually in <u>schools</u>, churches, and public buildings.

4. In the picture, some people are waiting to <u>vote</u>.

5. Today all American citizens <u>18</u> and older can vote.

6. Women and <u>African Americans</u> did not have the right to vote for many years.

7. In 1871, black men received the right to <u>vote</u>.

8. In <u>1920</u>, American women received the right to vote.

9. In 1984, a woman ran for Vice President, and she <u>lost</u> the election.

Understanding Sentences with Because (page 120)

2. e   3. b   4. d
5. a   6. f

Write (page 123)

2. African   3. women   4. citizens
5. secret   6. sex

CHAPTER 16 VETERANS DAY

Understanding New Words (page 127)

2. ceremonies   3. cemeteries   4. graves
5. bury   6. Tomb

Correct the Sentences (pages 128–129)

2. Americans bury many <u>veterans</u> in Arlington National Cemetery.

3. There are four special soldiers in this cemetery, and <u>nobody</u> knows their names.

4. The President or Vice President puts <u>flowers</u> at the Tomb of the Unknowns to honor all veterans.

5. World War <u>I</u> ended on November 11, 1918.

6. President Woodrow Wilson named November 11 <u>Armistice</u> Day.

Fact or Opinion? (page 129)

2. Opinion   3. Fact   4. Opinion   5. Fact

Write (page 131)

2. men

3. armed

4. Armistice

5. 1954

6. veterans

CHAPTER 17 THANKSGIVING DAY

Understanding New Words (page 135)

2. a

3. b

4. c

True or False? (pages 136–137)

2. True

3. True

4. True

5. False

6. False

7. True

8. False

9. False

10. False

Understanding Time Order (page 138)

2. The Pilgrims came to the United States on the *Mayflower*.
3. Many Pilgrims died during the first winter because they were sick and hungry.
4. The American Indians helped the Pilgrims grow food and build houses.
5. The Pilgrims and the Indians celebrated the first Thanksgiving.
6. Newcomers took land from the Native Americans and killed them.
7. People travel by plane, train, car, or bus for Thanksgiving dinner with relatives.

Talk About It, Activity 2 (pages 140–141)

2. In the morning, put the turkey in the oven.
3. Take the turkey out of the oven.
4. Call the family to the table.
5. Sit down to eat.
6. Eat the turkey.
7. Eat pumpkin pie.
8. Wash all the dishes.

CHAPTER 18 CHRISTMAS

Understanding New Words (pages 145–146)

2. needy

3. crowded

4. ornaments

5. greeting cards

6. jolly

7. carols

8. joyful

Correct the Sentences (pages 146–147)

2. The Christmas season starts after Thanksgiving, in late <u>November</u>.

3. Christmas is a time for giving presents to friends, family, and <u>needy</u> people.

4. Stores have beautiful decorations in Christmas colors of red and <u>green</u>.

5. Jewish people celebrate Hanukkah for <u>eight</u> days.

6. Greeting cards say, ''Happy <u>Holidays</u>,'' or ''Merry Christmas.''

7. During the weeks before Christmas, parents bring their children to see <u>Santa Claus</u>.

8. Children believe a fat, jolly man <u>brings</u> gifts on Christmas Eve.

9. Santa puts presents under the Christmas tree and in children's <u>stockings</u>.

10. Many Christians go to <u>church</u> on Christmas Eve or Christmas Day.

Talk About It, Activity 1 (page 148)

2. cemeteries

3. yellow

4. pizza

5. colored eggs

6. picnics